"Success means . . . havin[g] [a] job they make designer clothes for." Right!

"Is there life after Total Failure?" Hmmm . . .

After her childhood reputation as the Great Achiever wore off, Debra found the messes in her life too tough to handle. From the balcony railing, she counted the floors to the ground below.

Finish.

Then something happened.

"Oh God, what am I doing?"

Starting over meant learning that life is more than squeezing into designer jeans, or finding easy answers to problems like pain and depression. Fitness becomes an issue of belief as well as body. Is running a marathon really the greatest goal?

Debra had, quite literally, to take it over again: her approach to her job, her jogging, her friends, life and love, fat and fitness. But—Debra being Debra—nothing went quite according to plan.

Here is a book that talks about problems we all come up against. It's a book to make you laugh—and to make you think.

Debra Jarvis studied communications and Chinese at the University of California, Berkeley, and later theology at New College Berkeley. She worked as an aerobics instructor and in cardiac rehabilitation, and is currently training as a hospital chaplain. She is recently married and lives in San Francisco.

*This book is dedicated to Robert Edmiston,
my elementary school teacher who thought
nothing of giving his time, patience, love,
and encouragement to a 13-year-old girl
who wanted to write*

TAKE IT AGAIN FROM THE TOP

Life and love, fat and fitness

DEBRA JARVIS
works-it-out

A LION PAPERBACK
Tring · Batavia · Sydney

Copyright © 1986 Debra Jarvis

Published by
Lion Publishing Corporation
1705 Hubbard Avenue, Batavia, Illinois 60510, USA
ISBN 0 7459 1138 2
Lion Publishing plc
Icknield Way, Tring, Herts, England
ISBN 0 7459 1138 2
Albatross Books Pty Ltd
PO Box 320, Sutherland, NSW 2232, Australia
ISBN 0 86760 812 9

First edition 1986

Library of Congress Cataloging-in-Publication Data
Jarvis, Debra.
   Take it again—from the top.
   (A Lion paperback)
   1. Youth—Life skills guides—Anecdotes, facetiae,
   satire, etc. 2. Physical fitness—Anecdotes,
   facetiae, satire, etc. I. Title.
   HQ796.J3139 1986 646.7 86-169
   ISBN 0 7459 1138 2 (pbk.)

British Library Cataloguing in Publication Data
Jarvis, Debra
   Take it again—from the top.
   1. Adolescent psychology
   I. Title
   158'.1'088055   BF724
   ISBN 0 7459 1138 2

Cover photo: Wesley Van Voorhis

Printed and bound in Great Britain by
Cox & Wyman Ltd, Reading

Author's Acknowledgement

No man or woman is an island; I think we're more like connected pieces of land. That held especially true for me as I wrote this book. Many thanks to Walt and Ginny Hearn for their faith in me, their encouragement, their time, and endless cups of hot tea. Their editing skill, sense of humor, and prayers were invaluable—in other words, I couldn't have done it without them. Thanks also to my friend Dianne Peterson for encouraging me so thoroughly and sincerely through many long-distance phone calls. Most of all—thanks be to God for his faithfulness and for connecting me to such special pieces of land.

CONTENTS

THE GREAT ACHIEVER

I was the oldest, so I was *supposed* to be the Achiever.

Where did it start?

When I was seven years old I was the Big Star in a school play. It hurt when kids said I didn't fit the part: how could such a chubby Good Fairy fly? When I was eight it didn't matter what shape I was when my "Brush Your Teeth" poster took first prize. By the time I was twelve I was studying Chinese, probably just to show everybody how smart I was. At thirteen I won second place in a Chinese language speech contest. Gung ho Debbie.

But that was only one side of my life. The other side was often miserable. I was fat and my face was broken out. I was a mess, literally. I hated being clumsy. I hated being told all the time that I was too loud.

Reading was a big part of my life while I was growing up. I used to retreat from my childhood loneliness into fictional worlds. For a long time I read a book a day. Somewhere I had heard the phrase, "cultivating the mind." I used it to defend myself. When my mother chided me to go outside and play I would look up at her over my blue-rimmed, thick-lensed glasses and say, "Mother, I'm cultivating my mind." I'd get her I-don't-know-what-I'm-going-to-do-with-you look, but usually she would let me alone.

Alone was what I was a lot of the time. "Bookworm" was the only nickname I liked being called. "Big-mouth" and "Bull-of-the-woods" would send me shivering with hate and anger, but I wore "Bookworm" as a badge of solitary accomplishment.

My mother finally took me to a dermatologist to get my face cleared up. She also got me contact lenses, and soon I learned how to walk through a door instead of into it.

By high school I had made a profession out of being an Achiever. Class treasurer, newspaper reporter, varsity cheerleader. The whole image that I tried so hard to create was partly to make up for my not having many dates. Most boys I liked said I laughed too much. They thought I was "weird." Well, nuts to them. I had some girlfriends I got along with fine, thank you. We did all kinds of things together—throwing beach parties, Christmas caroling, getting drunk.

That made up for a lot, but during my senior year in high school I had a kind of foreboding that life would soon be going downhill. When I was handed my diploma I had the feeling that *THE END* had just flashed across the screen.

I was right. Everybody else at the University of California, Berkeley, seemed to fit in. But I hated it all—not even the macho football heros could raise a cheer in me.

For one thing, it was hard. From the time I decided to study Chinese, the Great Achiever was in trouble. It had been fun to make "A"s in high school and have my parents brag about me. My dad told everybody I was going to be the US Ambassador to China. The relatives always wanted me to say something in Chinese. Big deal. I'd say, "Hello. How are you? I'm fine." Sometimes I'd get fed up with being ambassador to China. Then I'd say something like "You are an American rat" in Chinese and tell them it meant "Have a nice day." It gave me a sense of power.

My sense of power didn't last long at the university, though, where some hotshots were studying both Chinese *and* Japanese *and* were applying to medical school at the same time.

Having lost its novelty, studying Chinese didn't do much for my social life either. Or my creativity. It wasn't the kind of subject you would sit up all night talking about. I was doomed to sit in my room and write characters over and over again—about as exciting as memorizing the local phone book.

I did make a few friends, but when we sat up late and talked it was usually over cups of coffee and chocolate chip cookies—dozens and dozens of chocolate chip cookies. That equation added up to one depressed Chinese student who gained twenty-two pounds . . . and became a caffeine addict.

In a burst of spirit the next year, the Great Achiever went out for the Women's Cross Country Team, but pretty soon even running couldn't get me out of my depression. I was lugging that extra twenty-two pounds around with me and I couldn't keep up. The other team members would drop back and run with me—when they had cramps or an injury. Somehow I managed to discipline myself to keep at it through my college years. Every day I would haul my body out of bed and run the dirt trails of Strawberry Canyon in the hills above the campus, usually alone. It was a challenge. "I may be fat," I would say to myself with my teeth clenched, "but I can run these six miles."

In one sense my running was a blessing that kept me going. At least I didn't gain more than twenty-two pounds. In another sense it was a curse. It was full of curses. With each pounding step I would curse the system —the educational system, the government, the housing set-up. I swore at my decision to study Chinese and I cursed my existence. I cursed the hills I was climbing. When I got to the top of the fire trail I was too tired to curse any more. Triumphantly I would look out over the panorama of San Francisco Bay. It was a physical triumph but there was no spiritual exhilaration in it. It was more like a defeat, in fact. It made me think of the emptiness of the rest of my life.

Things fell apart on a clear Fall day at the beginning of my senior year. I had spent my entire summer vacation in an intensive language course, studying eight hours a day. To get the fifteen units of academic credit that I needed I literally ate, drank, and slept Chinese. I had rice and tea for breakfast each morning. I started dreaming in Chinese. Two weeks after that course ended I was back in a regular Chinese class at the university.

That's when it happened.

The professor asked a simple question and called on me. I stared at her. She repeated the question. I kept staring. A classmate was pointing to the answer in my open book. Chinese characters were fighting a Tong war in my head. I could feel a flush spreading up from my neck to my ears. The class was silent, their eyes on me. I looked down at my book. Nothing. The professor asked me something else in Chinese but I couldn't understand her. My mind had gone blank.

My heart was pounding so loudly I knew everyone could hear it. I looked around the room. I had to get out. I slammed my book shut and with a sob bolted out of the room. A classmate told me later that I looked like a frightened fox surrounded by the hounds.

"Maybe you're just burned out," she said. "Why don't you drop by the student counselling service?"

I made an appointment that day. In the waiting room I looked around at the other students. What were they here for? Did that tall red-headed guy fall apart in Chem 1A and try to drink his experiment? Was that nervous-looking girl a philosophy student who found she could no longer sort Sartre?

My counselor was the portly type whose neck runneth over his buttoned-down collar. He folded his hands on his desk and leaned toward me.

"Now, what can we do for *you*?"

"I hate what I'm studying."

"Oh, you can't hate what you're studying. It's your senior year."

"But I do. I hate what I'm studying. It isn't satisfying to me. It isn't fun. I don't think I'm any good at it." My voice was beginning to shake.

"Now, now. Don't worry. I think you should talk to one of the psychiatrists on our staff. He could work with you . . ."

I jumped to my feet, dropping my backpack full of books to the floor with a thud. "I'm not *crazy*! I just hate what I'm studying. Can't you understand? You're the one who should see a psychiatrist!" I stood there defiantly, until I realized that I did indeed look like a crazy person. Crazy people never think they're crazy, I knew. I backed out of the room, smiling. "You're right. I *am* crazy. Guess I'll be running along now."

I ran out of the building before he had a chance to respond. Without a moment's hesitation I went to the office of the College of Letters and Science and filled out the forms to withdraw for the quarter.

That was the easy part. The hard part was telling my parents. I phoned them.

"How could you do this to us?" my father stormed. "Nine years of Chinese and now you quit. What am I supposed to tell my friends? I'm so ashamed."

"But Dad, I hated Chinese. It was killing me. I felt like I was losing my mind."

"I think you *have* lost your mind," he snapped. I hung up thinking maybe he was right. The Great Achiever had blown it.

My sister Lynie seemed to be the only family member who had any faith left in me.

"Don't worry," she said one night when I called her, "you'll find something you like. Dad will get over it. Besides, now maybe he'll start bragging about *me* for a change. Today I managed to cut the dog's toenails without getting scratched. That's something to brag about."

Lynie has a low-key sense of humor that she's never gotten enough credit for. I remember one time when somebody commented on her shyness: "Lynie is so quiet and reserved. I can't believe you two are sisters."

"Actually we're not," Lyn muttered under her breath to me, "we're brothers." Lyn could crack me up any time I was down. Like the time I smashed the car. And the time I spilled India ink on my mother's gold carpet.

"Why don't you just spill ink spots all over the carpet? We can claim it's leopard skin," she whispered, kneeling next to me as I tearfully scrubbed at the awful blot. Even in the worst situations, Lynie was a comic comfort to me.

My parents' friends would ask, "How could two girls brought up so close together be so different?" On the outside we *were* that different: she was always Skinny Lynie and I was Flabby Debbie; Lynie was graceful, thin, and quiet, but I was clumsy, fat, and noisy. On the inside, too, we had different needs and strengths, but we grew up filling the gaps in each other. As those inside gaps were filled we saw ourselves as a lot alike.

By the time we were adults we called ourselves "soul-mates." As children we didn't have a sophisticated term for it, but we knew that when we were apart for more than a day we both felt lonely. Not that we never fought. We were normal kids, tooth and claw. Mom still has a photographic portrait of Lynie with her hands demurely covering one side of her face. The day before, I had scratched a sizeable chunk out of it.

In high school I went for the wild, flashy boys. Lynie liked the ones who were sweet and nice and "quality" (as my mother would say). But the summer after graduation, a quality guy named Dan began to ask *me* out. The phone would ring, Lyn would answer, and it would be Dan calling for me.

"Tell him I'm not home," I'd whisper.

"But he's so nice. He's such a sweet guy," she'd whisper back.

"I don't care. He's not my type."

If Dan came by unannounced I'd sneak out the back door and leave Lyn to deal with him. Somehow she never complained. By the middle of the summer he started asking for Lyn instead of me. Four years later, when they announced their engagement, I was delighted. Once I realized he wasn't after me, I had grown to appreciate Dan. Besides, how could I dislike someone who was making my sister so happy?

At Dan and Lyn's wedding I shed tears of joy for them. Then I started shedding tears of sadness for myself. Lynie, my little sister, wouldn't always be around any-more. Someone else would now be her closest friend and confidante. Her first allegiance would now be with her husband. They were so obviously in love that it was like a fairy tale.

Most fairy tales have a witch lurking around somewhere. As everyone at the reception watched Lyn and Dan cut their wedding cake, one of my aunts nudged me. Her whisper had a kind of rasping sound to it: "That would be you up there now if you'd played your cards right."

I stared at my aunt in amazement. She wasn't making a little joke, however insensitive. She was serious. In her view, a charming younger sister had stolen the older one's boyfriend. To try to deny it would just make it worse. I swallowed and said, "Doesn't Lyn look beautiful?"

When I told Lynie what my aunt said she summed it up neatly: "Don't worry," she said, "she's like that. You have other things going for you. I'm excited about *your* life."

After Chinese and my "great leap backward," I finally graduated with a degree in Communications. Lyn cheered me on. She continued to cheer when I landed my first real job in the real world.

I became a "production assistant" for a small film company, or at least that's what I told people. What I really did was answer the phone, type letters, and make coffee. Pots and pots of coffee. But I could impress my friends by dropping terms like "dichroic," "cove cyc," and "day for night" into a conversation. I babbled on about flags, scrims, fingers and dots, gaffers, grips, DP's and spots.

I never told my family or friends about the porno companies that came in to use our facilities. I never said how much I hated the horrible things that happened on stage then, or revealed how blasé I was getting about it. I made my job sound full of glamour and excitement. That's what I wanted it to be.

The fact is that I was bored and disgusted. Eventually I started making up things to do to amuse myself. One afternoon I jokingly pretended to read aloud a memo I had just typed for my boss.

"Here's the list of things to do," I said with mock seriousness: "Blow up house; get rid of wife and kids; get haircut and shave." I looked up and laughed, but my boss wasn't laughing. Neither was his wife, who had just walked in to meet him for lunch. Oh well, I shrugged. Weak sense of humor, I thought to myself. Forget it.

Next morning the boss called me into his office. I pulled my chair up to his desk. I'd been hoping he would let me go out on location, or be script girl on the next shoot.

"Well, Deb," he said, "I'm going to have to let you go."

"You are? Great! On this next shoot? What will I be doing?"

He put his face in his hands and blew out a large puff of air. "You don't understand. I have to *let you go*—from your *job*." He might as well have told me I was going to be the next Pope.

"What? Let me *go*? You mean I'm fired?" He cringed when I said "fired."

"I hate to do this but I have to. It's difficult to explain . . ." He shook his head and his voice trailed off. "You simply have to be more careful about who you make jokes in front of. My wife was very upset. She . . . she just didn't understand."

"Didn't understand what?"

"She thinks . . . " He waved his hands absently in the air. "She thinks that you and I . . . that we . . ."

"That we *what*?" I practically screamed in his face. I was still too astounded to be hurt or angry.

"She thought we were fooling around." He said it fast, in a rush of words.

"You and I? But didn't you tell her that it wasn't true? Didn't you tell her I was only joking? Didn't you . . ."

He cut me off.

"You don't understand. She said she would take the kids and leave if I didn't fire you. And she would. She really would."

"I see." I stood up and put my hands on his desk and

leaned very close to his face. "Would you like me to finish out the week?"

"No, no. That's all right. We'll pay you for the rest of the week anyway."

"Thank you," I said numbly. I walked out of his office and back to my desk. I sat down, staring straight ahead. Was I dreaming? It was like watching myself on TV. Indignation and fury began to rise in me.

But wait a minute. Could I possibly have done something that wrong? If so, if I was the one who was wrong, I must call my boss's wife and apologize. I picked up the telephone, my fingers shaking. I dialed the number and waited for what seemed like a lifetime.

"Hello, Connie? This is Debbie." Silence. I thought maybe one of the kids had picked up the phone. "Hello? Can I talk to your mommie, please?"

"This is Connie." The ice in her voice came through the receiver and froze my fingers.

"Connie, hi. I'm calling to apologize. There must be some misunderstanding, so I just wanted to call you and apologize."

"Apologize? There can be no apology from you. You deserve everything you get." Her words were no longer cold but hot and furious, spilling out like burning lava into my ear. "I don't feel sorry for you one bit. So don't try to get your job back by calling me."

"Look, you don't understand. I didn't mean . . ."

"And why do you want to blow up our house? I never did like you anyway. This was Jack's decision and he's very glad he did it. He should have done it long ago!" The words kept coming faster and her voice kept getting higher. I tried to interrupt.

"But Connie . . ."

"Shut up!" She was getting hysterical. "I never did like the way you ran things over there. You'd say, 'Oh, hi, Connie, let me get Jack for you,' as if to say, 'What in the world are *you* calling for?' And why do you want to blow up our house?"

I sat there, tears streaming down my face and onto the

17

receiver, smearing the emergency police number and dripping down between the little buttons. I'm going to electrocute myself, I thought.

"Goodbye, Connie," I said, trying not to sob. The last thing I heard her scream into the phone was, "Jack is a very dedicated husband and moral person!"

That was my farewell to film-making. Nobody came to my desk to say goodbye. I took my *Doggone Dogs!* calendar off the wall, cleaned out my desk, and packed up my coffee mug. I would talk to Personnel about my severance pay some other time. For now I would just slip quietly away.

The next ten days slipped quietly away, in fact. I took valium by day and Jack Daniels by night. I had to drink to fall asleep because I was afraid to face my nightmares. Connie was always shooting me or stabbing me in them. I was strung out all day long. In a few days I finished off the valium prescription I'd been given for a torn muscle during college. Running would have been my salvation. Only now I couldn't even do that.

My parents didn't know the shape I was in but they knew I had failed again at something important. Disappointment was in their eyes when I drove home to tell them about it. They tried to be sympathetic but we all knew that their Great Achiever had once again blown it. Were they wondering how *they* had failed? In the long run it was they who decided that I should fly to Hawaii to stay with Lyn and Dan for awhile. They would have given me the trip for my graduation if I hadn't landed that "terrific" job with a San Francisco film company.

How ironic, I thought as I leaned over the balcony of my sister's Hawaiian highrise. The Great Achiever, a Failure. That's it, a Total Failure. I've failed at everything, I thought.

I peered down through the blackness to the parking lot. Well, I would fail just once more, and then no one would ever have to worry about my failing again.

It would be like the sprint at the end of a race, I thought, leaning out over the railing. I counted the stories down to the parking lot. A little push to get started, then faster and faster and whammo, the finish line. Finish is the right word for it. Finish this whole mess of my life.

"Hello, asphalt. Hello, blacktop. I'm coming to see you," I whispered. No answer came from the great black swamp. It was ready to swallow me.

The aroma of plumeria blossoms rose all the way up to the little balcony of Lynie's apartment, masking the smell of car exhaust. Darkness hid the flowers from me far below. I looked across to Manoa Valley but no twinkling lights flickered a greeting. Colorful Hawaii wasn't very colorful at that time of night. The valley seemed swallowed up by a great prehistoric swamp. And that swamp seemed so black, so encompassing, so . . . godless. "Godless" was a word that stuck in my mind.

My sister's soft voice interrupted the pounding going on inside my head. She and her husband were reading to each other in bed on this hot Hawaiian night.

I fingered the lei around my neck, given to me that evening. I had gone to the meeting only to please Lynie and to avoid spending time alone watching TV. It was a prayer meeting. People greeted me with handshakes, hugs, and leis. Then they started praying. People prayed for friends with cancer, strokes, paralysis. That made me nervous. I was perfectly whole physically but I knew I was the sickest person in the room. My whole being was like an open wound. I sat there aching, infected, rotting. Even Lynie couldn't comfort me this time.

"It's like a mercy killing. It'll be euthanasia," I whispered again into the darkness. My parents could say I'd been under intense mental strain. "So much potential," people would say, and then sadly shake their heads. Mental turmoil, even insanity, means that no one can be blamed. No one is responsible.

I swung my leg over the railing. I sat there perfectly still, feeling peaceful. It would be quick. Almost like flying. Only I'd rather fly in the clear blue California sky.

Another whiff of plumeria brought me back to the dark

balcony. What am I doing? I wondered. Does this rambling on mean that I'm about to go through with it? Is my whole life going to flash before me, the way they say it does?

"Oh God," I whispered to the godless darkness, "let's get on with it."

I hesitated an instant. I looked up and saw a single small star. Maybe that was God, waiting for me to die.

"Okay, Jesus," I said mockingly. "If you're out there you better come right now because I'm tired of living." I waited. The black swamp waited, expectantly. "Please, Jesus," I begged.

What happened?

I don't care what you call it—a religious experience, emotional exhaustion, sleepwalking—but Jesus did come to me.

I have been here all the time. You've just chosen to look the other way, he said. I could almost feel the physical comfort of someone caring for me, putting their arms around me.

The words came: "Jesus is here with me." I knew it was true.

I swung down off the railing and knelt down on the balcony. Huge, wrenching sobs escaped from me. I was crying as I had never cried before. Twenty-four years' worth of insecurity, loneliness, and self-hate poured out. I peeked through the bars of the railing down at the parking lot. The great black swamp looked angry. I was horrified at what I had almost done. That one small star was still twinkling above my head. I stared up at it through my tears. God was waiting for me to live, not die.

How long was I down on my knees? I don't know. Back inside the apartment I noticed that my salty tears had left brown spots all over the delicate petals of my lei. I lifted it gently over my head and went to bed. I didn't have to say everything to God that night. I knew that for the first time in weeks I would sleep a real sleep. Tomorrow I could pray again. I could keep on praying. And I could run. I could keep on running. I was back in the race.

 **Checkout**

1. Is there life after Total Failure?

- ☐ Yes
- ☐ No

2. Success means:

- ☐ getting good grades
- ☐ having perfect skin
- ☐ feeling comfortable wearing a bikini—in public
- ☐ having a foxy* boyfriend
- ☐ having **any** boyfriend
- ☐ hearing my name mentioned in the same sentence with Zola Budd and/or Billy Jean King
- ☐ having more friends than would fit in my house
- ☐ having the kind of job they make designer clothes for

    *foxy: adj., extremely good-looking, attractive

3. I find my identity in:

- ☐ my haircut
- ☐ my favorite rock group
- ☐ how people treat me
- ☐ what my parents tell me
- ☐ the kind of car I drive
- ☐ my wallet
- ☐ all of the above

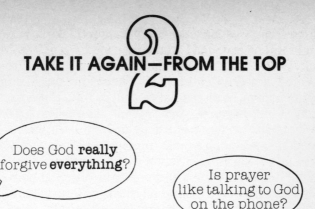

TAKE IT AGAIN—FROM THE TOP

Does God **really** forgive **everything**?

Is prayer like talking to God on the phone?

Will God hear me if I pray with my eyes open?

I didn't tell Lynie everything that had happened on her balcony. I simply said that I had decided to turn my life over to God, since I'd been making such a mess of it. For the first time in weeks she saw me smile. As we hugged each other she could tell how serious my decision had been. Then I asked her where we could go running that day. That clinched it. Lyn knew I was on the road to life, and pretty soon we were jogging together around a Honolulu track.

Lyn was in better condition than I was, physically as well as spiritually. She was striding easily next to me, chatting about how to live as a Christian. "You need to spend some time every day talking with God," she said, wiping a trickle of sweat from her face. It was early but already hot. My shirt was soaked through after only a half mile. I was waiting for my sweat to evaporate and cool me down in the Hawaiian morning sun. But the humidity enveloped my body like a sheet of plastic wrap.

"I'm suffocating," I panted, "but let's keep going." I found it difficult to talk. I was used to running alone.

Before my dramatic encounter with Jesus, running had been my salvation. It was my private time to recharge, reason, and respond. In public I always tried to come up

23

with a funny response to everything to make my friends laugh. But on my runs I would respond to things the way I really felt. Anger, hurt, humiliation all came out as I sweated and grunted up hills. They came out in smooth rhythmic breaths on the flats and in gasps as I reached the top of a hill. Running was the only time I didn't have to worry about being accepted by anyone. Lyn had always accepted me, though, and running with her on my first morning as a (gasp) Christian was sheer (pant) joy. Well, almost. I knew my life was going to be different now and I suspected that my running might be different, too.

When I returned to Berkeley after one month in Honolulu, I was ready to face the world again. I was coming back with a friend who would never betray me or leave me. I returned to the mainland with Jesus. Aloha.

I took seriously Lynie's advice about talking with God every day. My first week back in Berkeley I tried to sit at my desk and pray. That seemed too formal, even boring. I think my negative associations with desks and school got in the way. I thought maybe I could drop into some church every day and pray there, but that wasn't practical. Praying in bed was definitely a loser. I would fall asleep and then wake up guilt-ridden, ashamed that I had snoozed in God's company. How rude!

I was pondering this prayer problem one morning as I rounded the first corner of my run. "I give up, God. I just can't find a good time to talk to you. Nothing is working. I—oh, here's that hill. God, could you give me a little push up it, please?" Over the hill I ran, past the houses and tennis courts and then up into the hills along the fire trails. The morning dew coated the ferns and trees along the path with a velvet fineness. I found myself wondering how anyone could miss the evidence of a divine creator.

"You're everywhere, God. I see you in the rising sun and in the trees and flowers. I hear you in the insects buzzing past me. I feel you moving in my shadow on the ground." I ran on, talking the whole time, pointing out little things to God, bringing up my fears, questions, insecurities. I arrived home thinking that it was the best run I had ever had in my whole life. Why? I wondered. I attributed it to a good night's sleep the night before.

Forty-five minutes later, after a shower, I was making coffee for my friend Hammersly. We're pretty close, though we've always called each other by our last names. I wasn't sure she would understand, but I had told Hammersly about what happened to me in Hawaii. Now she was reading the paper and talking about some woman who gave birth to five babies after taking a fertility drug.

"They should be working on better birth control instead of fertility drugs," she snorted in disgust. "I wonder if anybody'll ever come up with a really *good* method of birth control."

I dropped the coffee jar on the table.

"Jogging!" I shouted, as it suddenly dawned on me that I had been praying all morning. Hammersly looked at me skeptically.

"Jogging? For birth control? You mean you should whip on your shoes and shorts and shoot out the door the minute you . . ."

"No, no! Jogging—that's when I can pray. I can't believe I never thought of it before."

Hammersly shook her head. "I don't know why you can't pray like normal people do." Hammersly can be sarcastic, but I was too excited to notice. It can be done, I thought. I could have my old salvation, running, and bring my new salvation with me.

After Hawaii I had gradually worked up from one mile a day to two and three and then four. Now every mile was ten minutes more I could spend talking with God. I ran in the early morning without minding the chill. I wore my hair tucked up under a baseball cap with a big bill that kept the spring showers out of my eyes.

I was also trying to read my Bible daily. I realized that in the same way that all cars and major appliances have instruction manuals, I did too—the Bible. And so, just as I read the instructions before trying out my food processor, I read scripture. Every day. I thought of reading the Bible like eating food—I didn't eat a huge meal to last for the rest of my life (only at my mother's!), I ate a little bit every day. Same with reading scripture. And even after I had read through the entire Bible, when I re-read it, different things jumped out at me. God spoke to me. The Bible was his Word and that's one of the reasons I found it so exciting.

When I came across chapter twelve, verse twelve of the letter to the Hebrews I was sure God was speaking directly to me: "Therefore strengthen your feeble arms and your weak knees." I began doing push-ups. Religiously, you might say. But I had another bible, too: *Runner's World* magazine. I read each issue cover to cover in one sitting. I bought shoe glue, knew about waffle treads, and named my Datsun B-210 after Bill Rodgers, king of the Boston marathon.

My entire life, physically, mentally and spiritually was awakened. Knowing God was the key. The change was like suddenly switching from black-and-white to color TV.

Besides running, the activity that took up most of my time after I got back from Hawaii was job-hunting. I was determined never to go back to the film world, but what could I do? I had always been interested in science, especially medical science. When everybody else was choosing courses in school like drama and synchronized swimming, I was taking anatomy and physiology. I hadn't been dedicated enough to try for medical school, but now I began to think about getting a job on the fringes of medicine. I decided to apply for a hospital job.

The most painful part of job searching is selling yourself. To sell anything, of course, it's important to believe in the product you're selling. That can be hard—especially if you were fired from your last job. Sometimes it was hard to remember that I was made by God to be the unique person that I am, and that I was really, truly, precious to him. At first it was hard to believe that I didn't have to *do* anything to earn his love. But he loved me through people —their kindness, understanding and compassion. And he loved me through the beauty of his creation. And he loved me as his spirit lived in me. Before every interview I would pray during my run: "Father, I know I'm okay because you made me. I get my self-worth from you because Jesus Christ is living in me, right? Please help me to remember that."

My first hospital interview was in the respiratory therapy department. The job available wasn't particularly exciting—filing, and answering the phone—but it was a job. The chief respiratory therapist was tall and thin. So was his hair. It stood straight up in stiff, gray columns toward the back of his head, a salt-and-pepper army retreating over the top of his skull. Atten-shun!

"I see you can type," he said, in command.

"Oh, uh, yes sir, I can type." He continued to pore over my job application as though he was about to sign the Magna Carta. His teeth were square and yellow with a space between each one, like the top of an old castle wall. He wore silver aviator glasses with thick lenses. Very thick lenses. They made his eyes look like billiard balls at the bottom of two water glasses. He finally looked up.

"Do you know anything about respiratory therapy?"

"No, not really. I . . ."

"Good. That isn't important. But I see you have a good background in anatomy and physiology."

"Yes, I . . ."

"Do you recognize that sound?" From down the hall I could hear a loud coughing, gagging, and wheezing.

I shook my head. "It sounds to me like someone coughing, gagging, and wheezing."

He nodded. "Yes, it's emphysema and that is Mrs. Henderson. People don't know how to take care of themselves." He pulled a pack of cigarettes out of his coat pocket and tapped one out into his hand. "That is the kind of disease I have to deal with every day and it isn't easy. Sometimes I don't know how I do it." He lit his cigarette with a polished marble lighter sitting on his desk. I had mistaken it for an ugly paper weight. He leaned back in his chair and blew out a large puff of smoke.

"What do you think of me?" he asked.

27

You're a dope, I thought to myself. I felt as if I had just found out that the friendly fireman on our block was moonlighting as an arsonist. I shrugged my shoulders. "I think you're probably used to it. It sort of goes with the territory." No sympathy from me.

"Hmmm." He glanced at my application again. "Frankly, I think you would be bored with this job. I'm afraid you're over-qualified."

I tried to look disappointed. "I understand. Thanks for your time." He waved my application at me as I turned away. "I'll forward this to other departments. You never know what kind of help somebody might need."

What kind of help? That word "help" made it sound like I didn't know how to wash windows, as in "It's hard to get good help these days." I went home depressed and disgusted.

My next interview was in the outpatient department. They needed a receptionist at the front desk. The outpatient department did all the minor surgical procedures. My job would be to direct patients to their rooms, ask for specimens, and answer the phone. Surgery, even minor, appealed to me.

I wore my navy blue suit and white blouse to the interview. Those were my "safe" clothes. Whenever I was feeling insecure I liked to wear something conventional, an outfit that wouldn't pop open, wasn't too tight, and didn't have a safety pin holding something in place. So, having prepared myself during my morning run with God, and wearing my working-woman ensemble, I faced the department head.

She was about fifty, wearing a polyester dress with a bold geometric design in bright pink, green, and orange. Her outfit looked like a TV test pattern. I tried to concentrate on her face, which was all basic black, since I was getting dizzy looking at her dress.

"What makes you think you're qualified for this job?" she asked.

Nothing like getting straight to the point. "The job description says 'typing, answering phones, must be good with people, and able to work early a.m. hours.' Well, I'm able to do all those things. I've done them in other jobs. Plus I think this would be a really interesting place to work."

She picked up my resumé. "Berkeley graduate? And you want to be a receptionist?"

"I want a job."

She rolled her eyes. "Girl, how long you think you'll stay in this job? I've had other girls like you. They transfer out in three months and then I'm stuck with hiring and training another one. I don't have the time or the energy for that." She stopped and suddenly became very formal. "We've had many applicants for this position. I will call you if we decide to hire you."

Right, I thought, feeling put down. I wouldn't want you to waste any of your time or energy picking up the phone. Why don't you just hire two nine-year-olds so they can grow into the job and you won't have to hire or train anybody for ten or fifteen years? I stood up. "Thanks for your time. I hope I hear from you soon." Going home on the bus I wondered if I should start looking into other lines of work.

Well-meaning friends who were employed started bugging me with advice. "Why don't you just get a fast-food job at McDonald's?" they would ask. Or, "God isn't going to drop the perfect job in your lap, you know." I did know that. And I did look for work in other places. But something made me keep trying the hospital.

"Oh, God," I prayed as the cool morning air brushed past my face, "I know you're teaching me lessons now that can't be learned any other way. But why won't anyone hire me? Do I look fat? Do I come across as a smart aleck? What do people think of me?"

God almost always answered me, sometimes so clearly it was like a voice in my head. This time he told me to wait, to trust him. He wanted me to be concerned about what *he* thought of me. I did trust him—but try telling that to people who've watched you job-hunt for three months.

"Don't you think it's time for you to take *any* job you can find?" they'd ask.

"No. I've been praying about the whole situation and I don't think that's what God wants me to do. I think I'm going to get a job at the hospital. In fact, I just know it."

"You mean you've really prayed about it and asked God to help you get the right job?"

"Yes."

"And what did he say?"

"To wait and trust him."

People who doubted that running was a good time to pray were the most skeptical. "Are you sure you're listening carefully? Maybe the message is getting garbled. Why not try having your quiet time with God after dinner?"

"Why? Do you think there's less spiritual traffic in the evening?" (Such critics did not bring out the best in me.)

At the beginning of my sixth month of unemployment I received a call from the hospital laboratory. By that time I had been interviewed for almost a dozen jobs. They were either part-time or on-call jobs or I was overqualified or underqualified. Sometimes they just didn't like my face, I decided.

Choosing a job

Many times you don't have a lot of choice about the kinds of jobs that are available to you. But to find the job that you are most likely to enjoy and do well at, you need to ask yourself some questions.

- Do you like working with people or do you prefer to work alone?
- Does it bother you to do repetitive tasks?
- Does working with the public excite or terrify you?
- Do you work well under pressure?

If you've already had quite a few jobs, write down what you enjoyed most about each one. Can you find a common theme running through each one? For example, were they all out-of-doors? Mostly involving paper work? Lots of contact with people? Perhaps they all involved meeting deadlines. Knowing what you liked about each job will be a key in helping you choose your next one.

By now I didn't care what I wore. I put on strappy old sandals instead of my professional "classic-design" shoes. I got out my mid-calf flounced skirts with satin and lace on the hem. I pulled on my white crepe blouse with billowing sleeves and tied a bright red scarf around my neck. I might be underqualified but they couldn't say I was under-dressed.

The lab office supervisor was named Aggie. She could have been a perfect TV grandmother: neatly combed curly gray hair, sparkling blue eyes, and a crisp but friendly way about her. She looked directly into my eyes.

"Are you familiar with the job qualifications?"

Here we go again, I thought.

"Yes, typing, filing, ability to work under pressure, basic understanding of lab tests."

"Good. I see that you've read the job description. Now I'll tell you what the job is really about: dealing with sick and frustrated patients, typing and answering the phone simultaneously, asking for every specimen imaginable—blood, urine, stools and sputum. You'll have to put up with rude, insensitive doctors who order everything 'stat'—meaning 'I need it now! Why isn't it done already?' Worst of all, you'll have to put up with me when I'm tired, cranky, and at the end of my rope. Do you think you can handle it?"

I nodded. "One summer I worked in a camp with fifty twelve-year-olds and two weeks of continuous rain. I can handle it."

"Good." She glanced at my application again. "I see you graduated from Berkeley." I could see it coming. It came, but with a twist: "Obviously you're overqualified for this job. That's not my problem. If you get bored but prove yourself competent, there's a chance you could transfer to another position. I need someone who can do the job. If I hired people because they were no better than merely qualified, my department would run like the rest of this hospital. And that," she said, closing my file, "is something that I have nightmares about. When can you start?"

I had been so ready to deliver my usual "Thank you for your time, and I hope to hear from you," that it took me a few seconds to reply.

"Immediately. Or whenever you like. Thank you *very* much."

"Well, don't thank me yet. Wait until you've done this job for a month and then see if you feel like thanking me. Come in Monday morning at 7:30." She looked me over, then added, "Thank goodness, you're a cheerful dresser. I get so tired of high heels and suits."

I floated out of her office. Nothing garbled about *that* message, I thought. I grinned at what my friends had said, and sort of winked at God. I had the feeling that he winked back.

Aggie was in for a surprise. At the end of a month I did thank her. Not just for the job but for her friendship and

---

Going for the interview: what gives you confidence?

CLOTHES:
- **Don't** wear your favorite, most comfortable blue jeans unless you're interviewing for a stable-hand job.
- **Do** wear something that is neat, clean, makes you feel good about yourself and isn't held together with safety pins.
- Before your interview, check out what other employees are wearing—that will give you a clue as to what's appropriate.

WHAT TO SAY:
- First of all: **relax**
- Answer the questions honestly and keep in mind that they are looking for a person to fill a position—they are not "out to get you."
- Be aware that you may be asked questions like, "Why do you want this job?" "Where do you see yourself in five (two, ten, twenty) years?" "What qualifies you for this position?"
- Don't be afraid to bring up relevant job experience. You're not bragging, you're simply stating the facts.
- Don't be afraid to ask your own questions. "Could you explain more fully what I would be doing?" "What is the salary?" "Will I be paid over-time?" "What kind of supervision will I have?" These are all fair questions and show the employer that you are serious about the job.

guidance. The job itself was easy and I settled into the routine.

Summer came. Sometimes, when I had to go to work early, I would run in the evenings around dinner time. Then I would encounter baseball games, dog walkers, and the smell of backyard barbecues. I always smiled and said "hi" and wondered if those people and dogs could see God running with me.

Before long I began entering weekend ten-kilometer races—just over six miles. The first time I ran with an official number pinned to my T-shirt I was like a kid on Christmas morning. All around me runners were stretching out, talking about their PR's (personal records), and comparing the various features of their running shoes. I felt like an honest-to-goodness athlete. I wished I could encounter the guy who had jeered at me when I was eight and an enthusiastic (if unspectacular) baseball player: "Don't let *her* up to bat. She can't even make it around the bases."

By the time I had improved my own PR for the 10-K by six minutes, I was "into running" in a big way. I bought all the running magazines. I had the latest in training shoes, the best in shorts, and the hottest in socks. With every race I added a T-shirt to my collection, emblazoned with the name of the race. Of course, since most of the races were on Sundays, there was less and less time for church.

It was a pleasant change to have everything seeming to go well for me. I was running faster all the time. My job in the lab seemed to be getting easier. I had hit my stride.

One Friday afternoon as I was about to leave work, a patient came into the lab demanding to know who "D.J." was. We had to initial every request for a lab test as we typed it up so that if a problem arose it could be traced to the source. I was the "D.J." who had typed up that request. I had checked the wrong test.

The man waved the slip angrily in my face. His fingers were fat and stubby. Long dark hairs grew out between his knuckles. His gold wedding band was cutting deep into his finger. I wondered if at one time, maybe on his wedding day, his finger had been smooth and thin.

"You ordered the wrong test. Now I have to get stuck with one of your stupid needles again. They ought to stick you instead."

People in the waiting area were looking up over their magazines. "I'm sorry, sir," I said sympathetically. "It was entirely my mistake and if you'll just take a seat I'll make sure that you are seen immediately."

"I don't care!" he shouted. He addressed the whole waiting room: "Does this hospital hire only morons?" Back to me: "Don't you have a brain in your head?"

A nervous diabetic and a very pregnant woman closed their magazines and stared openly. An old man in a wheelchair wheeled himself a little closer. I swallowed. "Sir, I'm sorry. It was a stupid mistake. I . . ."

"I'll say it was stupid. Don't you understand that I'm a sick man? Don't you realize that I'm suffering? Maybe you should go back to first grade with the other six-year-olds."

That did it. Who was this jerk anyway? I didn't have time for that kind of garbage. I had to get home and put in my four miles. "You sure are sick," I said. "What are you suffering from—terminal rudeness?"

At that point Aggie walked up, saw what was happening, and yanked me into her office. "Don't leave," she said over her shoulder as she returned to the front desk to smooth things over. Great, I thought, looking at my watch. There goes my run. I started pacing up and down. Why was she taking so long? I sat down, tapping my fingers on the desk, inspecting the photos of Aggie's grandchildren, and diddling with my hair. Oh, oh, I thought. Is this going to be a replay of a scene I've been in before?

When Aggie came in, she sat down quietly behind her desk and looked at me. She folded her hands and put them on top of the desk. I folded my hands and put them in my lap. She took in a deep breath, blew it out slowly, and leaned back in her chair. It's coming, I thought. I held my breath and stared intently at my class ring.

She didn't fire me. She didn't even blow up at me. She just said, "I'm really disappointed in you. I would have expected a little more self-control."

Her words hit me right in the Achilles heel of my emotions. I wished that she had gotten angry and called me an idiot. Her disappointment was harder to take. It meant that I had let Aggie down. I had failed again, and let somebody down that I cared about.

Aggie stood up. "You can go." That was all she said. She walked out and left me sitting there. I didn't feel like running anyway.

The next morning I woke up depressed. It was Saturday and I could run in the middle of the day. I ran ten miles along the park trail that leads up to Inspiration Point. What possessed me to do such a foolish thing? I had never run more than 6.2 miles before, and had never run even that distance in the midday sun. Running along that dirt trail with the tall grasses and trees suffocatingly still in the shimmering heat, the dust exploded beneath my feet with each step. I could feel a thin coating of salt on my face from the sweat. My cotton shirt clung to me, heavy and wet. I thought about the apostle Paul, and how, before he became a Christian, he'd met Christ in a dazzle of blinding light on the dusty road to Damascus.

No other runners were in sight on such a scorching day. I saw an occasional lizard on the trail. It would pop out, blink painfully in the bright sun, then scurry back into the shade. I hadn't thought to bring a water bottle, or even a hat. Now I was paying for it. I felt alone and abandoned.

"I'm so hot and tired, God," I prayed. "I don't think I can make it back." I couldn't say much more than that. My tongue was like a dry tortilla. I couldn't swallow. I was weak and dizzy by the time I got home. I collapsed exhausted on my front porch. It took me three tries to turn the spigot and get some water to flow from the garden hose. The warm water tasted of rubber. I almost gagged, suddenly thinking of bugs and slugs sleeping in there the night before. I threw down the hose in disgust and summoned up the strength to go inside.

I slumped into the sofa with a glass of iced tea and picked up some running magazines. I was combing back issues for articles on heat stroke and dehydration. A quote from a veteran distance runner jumped out at me: "You want to start out slow and build. You have to prepare and you'll have days where you just don't feel strong. But your daily preparation, your daily training, will carry you through."

My daily training? I hadn't read my Bible in weeks or had any real Christian fellowship. When I had occasionally made it to church my mind would wander and I would miss the whole point of the sermon. I had been so busy trying to run farther and faster that I had gotten careless about talking to God.

I dropped the magazines onto the coffee table and went searching for my Bible. I could barely remember where I had left off. Maybe in Ephesians? Yes, there were the verses I underlined in chapter six: ". . . be strong in the Lord and in the strength of his might. Put on the full armor of God, that you may be able to stand firm against the schemes of the devil . . . stand firm and having shod your feet with the preparation of the gospel of peace."

Preparation. A Christian has to prepare. A runner has to prepare. I had been caught unprepared. Running in ninety-degree noontime sun was pretty dumb. Forgetting to spend time talking and listening to God was pretty dumb. I learn slowly but I learn. I never again went running in the heat. And I never again went running without God.

 **Checkout**

PRIORITIES

PRAYER

It doesn't have to be a drag! Yeah, yeah, God does know everything that's on our hearts but it doesn't mean he doesn't want us to bring our joys and concerns to him. Besides that, you have to give him equal time—you know, spend some time listening. There's no formula for **how** to listen to God. (For me it's a feeling, a real peace I get about something.) God speaks to me as I read the Bible and through other people—in the advice they give me, or the story of an experience they've had. Sometimes he even speaks to me through a book I'm reading when I'm particularly struck by a word, or a sentence, or an idea. And what happens if he doesn't seem to answer? God answers all prayer—but not necessarily when or how we want it answered. "No" is an answer too. But we can trust that everything he allows is for our good.

SCRIPTURE

How should you live? Look it up—in the Bible. It really is like an instruction manual, or spiritual food that needs to be eaten and digested every day. The digestion part is important—think about what you've just read, meditate on it and even memorize it.

FELLOWSHIP

God also speaks to us through one another. Once we accept Christ, we are tied to all the other believers in him—we enter the spiritual "family" of Christ and we really do **need** each other. Spending time with other Christians, in addition to praying and reading the Bible, is one good way to help us understand what giving and receiving is really about.

YOU MEAN REAL PEOPLE GO TO CHURCH?

What does the word "church" mean to you?

☐ boredom
☐ loud organ music
☐ rummage sales
☐ a big building with a steeple
☐ a collection of odd bods
☐ stained glass pictures of saints
☐ lisping people who say "passeth," "saith," "thee," and "thou"
☐ a "family" of people who care for each other and worship together

I arrived at Susy's door for dinner, face still flushed from the six miles I had put in on the trails, hair still wet and stringy from my shower. I was looking forward to a good meal. Nothing like a long, hard run to make me feel justified in "porking out." Burning off about a hundred calories per mile meant that I could eat two pieces of apple pie, a half pound of spaghetti with meat sauce, or fifteen small chocolate chip cookies—and it wouldn't matter at all.

We sat at a great big round table covered by a red-checked tablecloth, like in an Italian restaurant. The tablecloth even had little stains on it, from a long-forgotten lasagna or a drip of pasta past. Susy was fond of Italian food. Come to think of it, that's all I remember ever eating at her place. But, *buono*!

She had collected quite a crowd that night: a doctor from Massachusetts, a medieval literature teacher, an electrical engineer, and myself, plus Susy and her husband Bruce. The conversation was lively, ranging from "Does Princess Diana clean the royal shavings out of the sink or does Charles?" to "Is white chocolate *really* chocolate?" I sat back, watching Susy laugh and talk. I was thinking of the first time I met her.

I had just returned from that month in Hawaii that had changed my life. I hadn't gone to Hawaii as a tourist, really, but my experience with Jesus Christ there made me realize that I'd been a kind of tourist all my life. Now that I belonged to God I was no longer merely a tourist or stranger in his world. Before I left Hawaii, my sister and brother-in-law stressed the importance of belonging to a church—a "family" that would care about me, love me, and make me feel needed. So I made a deal with God: I would go to every church in Berkeley and he would let me know which one I should join.

Being the new Christian that I was, I expected to have a dream or a vision. Or maybe I would find a ten-dollar bill in front of the church—which of course I would consider a sign from God. I decided to start closest to home. I would visit that ugly, sickly-green church on the corner where my bus always stopped. The building was hideous, but what the heck, it was a church. Looking back now I realize that I was pretty skeptical about God holding up his end of the bargain.

That Sunday dawned bright and sunny, which is pretty unusual for Berkeley in January. Hmmph, I thought to myself, there goes Plan B. I had subconsciously been hoping that the weather would be so bad I'd be forced to stay home. Maybe a sudden shower of hail? A flashy electrical storm? Even a freak tornado would do.

I started to get dressed. Aha! I bet I didn't have a pair of pantyhose. How could I possibly go to church without pantyhose? I yanked open my drawers with glee but there, under a mangled slip and one of those old stretchy hair-bands, I found a brand new pair. Rats. Every excuse I could think of failed. I wasn't out of coffee or dental floss, I didn't miss my bus, and I wasn't hit by a car while crossing the street. So in no time at all I was confronted by that green stucco monstrosity masquerading as a house of God.

I stood outside on the steps for a long time before going in. I was sure that I loved God. I just wasn't so sure that I loved going to church. In my childhood, church had meant going to Sunday school and coloring pictures of Jesus and the disciples, or getting sick from eating the white paste we used to make Easter cards. I hated sermons. My sister and I and our friends used to take up a whole pew. If you sat with your shoulder against the back and your rear slightly forward, there was just enough space behind you to roll a large cat-eye marble from one end of the pew to the other. The trick was to do it without laughing or jumping to your feet if it lodged beneath your dress. As I matured, I simply brought a *Reader's Digest* to church and read that during the sermons.

So I was more than slightly apprehensive as I walked up the steps. I slinked through the door spy-style: poking my head in first, looking cautiously left, then right, then slipping my body in and closing the door quietly behind me. To my surprise there was nobody in the lobby they called the narthex. In fact there wasn't anybody in the sanctuary. Then I noted the felt-board sign: *Sunday School, 10 a.m., downstairs. Worship Service, 11 a.m.*

I glanced at my watch. Oh, great. I came too early. I was not about to go downstairs and color pictures of Jesus with a bunch of four-year-olds. I looked around. Might as well kill time in the women's room. To this day I don't know what I thought I would do in there for an hour—wash my hands a few hundred times?

It was there that I ran into Susy—literally. I charged in, pushing open the door just as she was coming out. That combination resulted in a loud thud as Susy staggered back against the mirror, hand pressed to her head. Oh, no, I thought, maybe this is my sign from God—a sign to *leave*. Susy started laughing and stuck out her other hand.

"Hi, my name is Susy. I don't think I've met you before."

41

"Well, uh, gee, I'm sorry. I just wanted to kill time, not people. I came too early so I . . ."

"No, you didn't. Sunday school is just starting. Come downstairs with me. My father is teaching a class on Genesis."

"Oh, no! I mean I . . ." Before I knew what was happening she had me by the hand and was dragging me down the stairs to the class. Good grief, a Sunday school class on Genesis. I had visions of coloring pictures of Adam and Eve and getting sick on white paste.

Instead of a bunch of screaming kids, I was greeted by a group of friendly adults who introduced themselves to me and told me how glad they were that I had come. I sniffed suspiciously for paste breath but they were clean. To my surprise the discussion on Genesis was interesting. I was so nervous at the time that I can't recall now what we talked about. I do remember feeling eager to go home and read the next chapter to find out what happened.

Upstairs, the worship service was also different from what I had expected. Seated between my new friend and her parents, I knew they would notice if I started doodling on the pew cards. I resigned myself to having to pay attention. I looked around at the sanctuary. Standard-issue Protestant: no towering statues of Mary, no choirs of squatty candles burning, no intricately carved altar. The rows of smooth vanilla pews reminded me of lady-fingers delicately laid out on a plate.

The organ was small, like a home-style instrument. And the organist wasn't wearing a dramatic robe—just a dress and a soft smile. I remembered once being in a church where the organist was decked out in a purple and black robe with a piece of fur hanging over his shoulder. Everybody said it was ermine but to me it looked like a dead hamster. That guy had played the doxology like an audition for the New York Conservatory of Music. He swayed back and forth. He tossed his head like a horse at the starting gate. He got very emotional toward the end of a hymn and always played the "men" part of the "Amen" way too long. The whole congregation would run out of breath and you could hear everybody suck in air all at once. But this organist seemed calm, gently playing a quiet background piece.

I looked at the carpet running up the center aisle. Why did it look so familiar? I meditated on that for awhile. Then it dawned on me: sea-foam green, the same color as the outfits I'd had to wear for gym when I was thirteen. That gave me a vaguely uneasy feeling. I had never been an Achiever in PE.

I was waiting for some old man in a black robe and carrying a Bible to appear on stage. Instead the congregation was greeted by a young guy in a suit who looked far too pleasant to be the minister. We sang a few hymns and then he asked if anybody had a word of praise. Who was this guy? Some kind of grown-up altar boy? What did he mean, "word of praise"? A woman stood up and he called on her by name. Hmm, he knew her name. That probably meant that she was his girlfriend.

"I want to praise God for giving me a crabby boss. She is really hard to get along with, but this week God gave me a special love and understanding for her, and we've been getting along much better." She smiled and sat down. The man next to her put his arm around her and kissed her on the cheek. That shot the girlfriend theory.

Then an older woman got up. I wouldn't classify her as the "little old lady" type because she was much more dignified than that caricature. Her white hair was combed and pinned up so it swirled about her head like cotton candy. She was conservative with her makeup, not trying to hide years of worry, grief, or whatever with gallons of ivory foundation. Nor did she try to reclaim her youth with the newest shade of rouge painted in precise little circles on her cheeks. She was none of that. All I noticed was a little pink lipstick and silver-rimmed glasses. She was having trouble standing and I saw that she was gripping the head of a wooden cane, her knuckles white with the effort. Her other hand was clutching the pew in front of her.

"I want to thank God for my family," she said in a clear,

strong voice. "And by family I mean all of you. I thank him for getting me through my hip surgery and for all your prayers, cards, and visits. So many times when the pain seemed too much for me I would be bitter and angry and turn away from God." She paused and looked down. For a moment I thought she wouldn't be able to go on, but she straightened up and threw back her head. "Yes, so many times I—why, I almost hated him, but he would always send a brother or sister to me to remind me of his everlasting love." She paused again and a smile broke across her face that did more than rouge ever could. "And I want to thank him for the lessons in patience that he taught those who were with me. I know that it's not easy to spend time with a crotchety old lady like me."

A ripple of laughter passed through the congregation. A few people smiled knowingly and nodded. The man in charge leaned over the pulpit.

"We sure do love you, Anna, and we thank God for your example of courage and strength. God bless you."

"But pastor, that's what I'm telling you—he has, he really has." She sat down, fumbled in her purse, produced a delicate lace hanky, and dabbed at her eyes under her silver-rimmed spectacles.

I couldn't believe what had just happened. The young man was the pastor. And he talked *with* the people, not just *at* the people. It was the sort of thing that happened only at a family dinner table, between "Please pass the peas" and "Get your elbows off the table." Was this what Lyn and Dan meant when they talked about the "family of God"?

I had picked up the idea as a child that people spoke to the minister only at funerals or weddings. Our minister never seemed quite human to me. My sister had noticed it too.

"How come he never scratches?" she whispered to me one morning in church. "I've never seen him scratch himself *ever*."

"Don't you know *anything*?" I said with disgust. "He doesn't need to scratch. He's holy."

"Oh, yes," she said reverently. She sat up straighter in the pew and gazed at him with fascination.

Not long after that, our minister picked up a bad case of poison oak on a weekend retreat and subsequently lost all credibility with my sister and me.

And now, some twenty years later, I was sitting in a church where the pastor and the people were talking together during the service. He leaned forward on his pulpit once again.

"And now let us prepare to pass the peace."

Pass the piece? Oh no, are we doing communion? Am I supposed to pass the piece of bread to the next person? I didn't even see any bread. Oh, oh, I'm going to blow it.

But everyone stood up. I stood up, a little off cue. Susy gave me a hug.

"The peace of the Lord be with you."

"Oh, thank God," I said with a sigh of relief.

"Yes, praise the Lord," she said with a smile.

So "passing the peace" meant sharing the peace of Christ with others who believed in him. I sank gratefully back into my seat. I was feeling like one of those chihuahau dogs who yip and shiver and won't let you get close, but who are really dying to be petted. It was all so unfamiliar to me: the warmth in the greeting from a stranger, the humanity of the pastor, the closeness of the congregation. I was so overwhelmed by it all that I planned to sneak out right after the benediction.

Caught. Susy had put her arm around me. "Why don't you come to lunch with us?"

I started to whimper. If I'd had a tail, it would have been between my legs. This was back in the days when I didn't have a job and I was absolutely without a dime. I was mortified. What could I say, that my pocket was picked at church?

Susy waited for my answer, then squeezed my arm. "My treat, of course."

In true canine form, my mouth dropped open and it was all I could do to keep my tongue from hanging out. I pawed at her arm.

"Oh, thank you! I'd love to. What a surprise! How nice of you. Oh, boy!" I stopped as I realized that everyone staring at me was probably wondering if I'd just been offered the Hope diamond. I almost wished someone had shoved a bone in my mouth just to shut me up.

So, that Sunday afternoon, after the best crab sandwich and chocolate malt I'd ever had, I realized that Susy was my sign from God. Surely it was a miracle for Susy to be so nice as to buy me lunch after I had just about brained her with a bathroom door. So this must be the church he . . .

"Please pass the peas. And get your elbows off the table."

I was jerked back into the present by a nudge in the ribs from Susy. "Boy, you must have had some run. Maybe you're zonked out with 'runner's high.' I've asked you to pass the peas three times already."

I put down my forkful of spaghetti. "What? We're passing the peas?" I leaned over, put my arms around Susy, and hugged her. "The peas of the Lord be with you."

"Oh, no!" she groaned. Bruce hit me on the head with the serving spoon. The doctor from Massachusetts choked on his milk. The teacher and the engineer looked confused.

"That did it," Susy scolded me in mock seriousness. "No more running. It's getting to you."

I kept hugging her, my sign from God. I was thinking about my new "family" and how God had used Lyn and Dan and Susy to draw me into it.

"You're right, Susy. Something *is* getting to me. But it isn't running."

46

JUST THE SAME OLD ME?

Believing in God means:

☐ I'll have to start wearing a cross around my
  neck
☐ I can't have any fun
☐ having peace
☐ changing my personality
☐ I can't sleep in on Sunday mornings
☐ not having to make it on my own
☐ discovering new and exciting things about
  myself

"You've got two to do in intensive care and one in dialysis. The rest are on the floors."

"Okay. Thanks." I wheeled my EKG machine out the door and down the hall toward the elevator. After three months of working in the laboratory I had transferred to the cardiology department as a technician. This job was challenging and more interesting than trying to get patients to part with specimens.

This morning I had a light load, ten in all. Not too bad. I pushed the button for the elevator and waited. I felt stiff because I hadn't had time to stretch after my run. I looked around, then slowly reached for my toes with my legs straight. My hamstrings were tight. I pushed a little farther and got my hands flat on the floor. I could feel my legs start to loosen up.

"Are you going to spend the day examining your toe-nails or do you want to get on?" I straightened up to face an elevator full of people. A doctor was holding the door open.

"Oh, sorry." I pushed my machine in without looking at their faces. I stared at the floor, in fact. I was standing right next to the doctor and could see the gray cuff of his trousers hanging over his brown wing-tipped shoes. One shoe was tapping, tapping, tapping.

"Which floor do you want?" he said impatiently.

"Oh! Four, please." The doors slid shut with a sigh and we were on our way down. A phlebotomist standing beside me gave me a sympathetic smile. That's one job I wouldn't want. Phlebotomists, who go from room to room collecting blood, aren't exactly popular with patients. I've seen patients go into a restroom and never come out when they see that needle coming. Sometimes they dive under the covers or pretend they're in a coma. None of those ploys ever keep phlebotomists from making their appointed rounds, however.

My patients were much more agreeable. Take my first one that morning, Mr. Ingram. He was in for a bleeding ulcer.

"Look, sweetheart," he said. "Don't tell me it's another test. The only thing they haven't tested me for is my IQ, knock on wood. What's that thing for?"

"I'm going to do a . . ."

"Look, sweetheart, I've already had one of those. The doctor knows I had a heart attack two years ago. That's not what I'm here for. I'm here for this pickin' bleeding ulcer!"

No kidding, I thought to myself. From your antsy attitude I never would have guessed. But I said, "Now listen, Mr. Ingram. Let me tell you the truth. I'm not really an EKG tech. Actually I represent *Playgirl* magazine. I've come to see if you have enough hair on your chest to make it as a centerfold. I had to disguise myself to get in. Now, let me just put these electrodes on your chest, Mr. Ingram."

"Ha-ha! Call me Cliff," he roared. The curtains swayed with the force of his voice. "Do I qualify? Ha-ha! You're not gonna find a better forest than that!"

I smiled weakly. The electrodes weren't sticking because of all that thick, gray hair. Finally I got him hooked up. "Okay, all you have to do is relax," I said. "I do all the work."

"Look, sweetheart, that's what you're paid for!"

"Right. Now just be quiet and relax." Telling Mr. Ingram to relax was like commanding an ant hill to sit still.

"Aren't you done yet, sweetheart?"

"Not yet. I was almost done until you started talking. See, when you talk and move I get a lot of little squiggly lines like this." I held up the tracing for him to see. "That's called muscle tremor and the doctors don't like to see that on an EKG. They like the lines to be nice and smooth. So just keep your pants on and I'll be done in a second."

"Ha! Keep my pants on? I thought you were from *Playgirl* magazine!" That crack brought on mountains of guffaws and yuk-yuk-yuks. I was beginning to get tired of this.

"You know, Cliff, we can't use models who don't know how to cooperate." It was a lame line but it worked. He kept perfectly still. He looked deathly still, in fact, but my EKG training showed he was alive. I unhooked him and pulled off the electrodes.

"We'll notify you of our decision. Thanks a lot. Bye-bye." On to the next patient.

One reason I liked my job in cardiology better than the lab job was that the department was full of runners. The chief cardiologist was a marathon runner. Most of the office staff were runners and almost all the technicians were. I wasn't the only one who came in with wet hair in the morning. On our breaks we would sit in the lounge, sip coffee, and complain about shin splints, tendonitis, and fallen arches. Or rejoice over a perfect run, a new personal record, or a super pair of running shoes. It was fun to be with people excited about running. There was one problem, though. They kept wanting me to go on runs with them.

"Let's meet at Tilden Park after work and run the trails," they'd say.

But I'd rather run alone, I thought to myself. That's my

time to pray, to be with God. Instead I would say, "I can't. I have to meet a friend for coffee right after work."

"Bring your friend."

"Bring my friend? Oh, uh, my friend doesn't run."

Sometimes I did run with people in the department to keep them from asking too many questions.

"Don't you hate getting up to run in the morning? I don't know how you can stand it—especially running alone," they would say. I wanted to tell them that the world is a different place at six in the morning. In the cool air there's a sense of the great energy of the coming day, yet the people you meet are gentler, kinder, somehow more vulnerable. Everything around you seems to be holding its breath, waiting for daylight, quietly anticipating the sunrise. It's in that early stillness that God and I run the streets of Berkeley, jumping curbs, shushing barking dogs, dodging potholes.

I wanted my new friends to know about my morning runs with God, but I wasn't sure they would understand. So I said: "Oh, I'm just a morning person. You know how slow I run—nobody could stand to run with me anyway."

I guess it was inevitable that the runners in our department would want to run in a race together. Not just some obscure, unknown, weekend run. Everybody wanted us to enter the biggest race in the world, San Francisco's annual 7.6-mile Bay-to-Breakers race.

We decided to start training together Saturday mornings. We'd meet at the hospital and go up behind the Claremont Hotel where there were lots of hills to train on. Hills? Might as well run up Mt. Everest. But I was willing to give Mt. Claremont a try. We assembled at the entrance to the emergency room.

"How appropriate," Ed said. "We'll probably end up here after this run."

"Oh, Ed, quit being so pessimistic. I think it'll be a lovely run. It's a lovely morning and we're all in pretty good shape. Besides, you're the fastest runner here. What have you got to worry about?" Judy stood there scolding him, with her hands on her hips. She didn't look very intimidating in her fuzzy pink warm-up suit and baby-blue running shoes.

"Maybe Ed's right, Judy," Gina wailed. "What if we can't all make it? What if my ankle acts up again? Ed will probably just take off and leave us."

Ed sighed and looked annoyed. Gina always had something to complain about. As office manager she was always whining. Her frizzy black hair never stayed combed, so it looked like a collection of black blanket fuzz all stuck together. She had started running only six months before. After losing thirty pounds and working up to four miles a day, she was hooked.

I jumped into the conversation.

"Aw, c'mon, Gina," I said. "You know how slow I go. If you get tired I'll stay with you."

We took off single file up Ashby Avenue, busy even on a Saturday morning. Judy was running in front of me and every so often she would turn around and flash a smile and say "How ya doin'? Ya doin' okay?"

I'd nod and smile, but actually it annoys me when people leave the endings off of verbs. In my mind "doing" shouldn't rhyme with "ruin" as in "how ya doin'." I was already irritated at Judy, I guess—she couldn't have weighed more than ninety-six pounds and she's three inches taller than I am. She had never run a step in her life until she came to our department as a nurse and caught the running bug. She always wore pastels. Ugh, pastels. They're so indecisive. The color pink always tempts me to ask, "Well, which is it? Make up your mind—are you red or are you white?"

Judy is a platinum blond. She once told us that her mother had always dressed her in pastels to complement her "naturally blond" hair. Then Ed looked closely at her head and made a very nasty crack: "What color complements those naturally dark roots?" Judy turned a bright purple, the deepest color anybody's ever seen her in, and stormed out of the office. I was amazed that they were able to work together after that.

When Judy caught the running bug, she caught it bad. She bought everything you could possibly associate with running: shoes, shorts, socks, warm-ups. Today she sported a water bottle, a velcro wrist band to carry her gum in, and a pink visor to match her warm-up suit.

Ed. What was Ed's problem? He always had a word about everything. A sarcastic word.

After Gina had lost about twenty pounds, I said to Ed, "Doesn't Gina look great?"

"Yeah. She's gone from beached whale to hippo." Oh, Ed.

Occasionally Ed and I would have lunch together. "Ed," I'd say, "want to have lunch with me?"

"Sure. Better than getting poked in the eye with a sharp stick."

The weird thing was that everybody knew Ed didn't mean it. He would say outrageous things about patients: "Mrs. Pastorini would save us a lot of work if she'd just croak. Then I wouldn't have to smell her ravioli breath every time I'm in her room." But when we wheeled Mrs. Pastorini down to the lab for her angiogram I could hear Ed talking to her. "Don't worry. You're going to be fine. I'll be right next to you and if you get even a little scared, you can squeeze my hand." Ed was a mystery.

He was way ahead as we started to run up the road behind the Claremont. Just then Gina grabbed my arm. "My ankle. I think my ankle is starting to hurt."

I laughed. "You *think* it's starting to hurt? Well, why don't we just keep running and see for sure? Maybe it just needs to be warmed up."

After a few minutes of silence, Gina spoke again. "How come you never want to run with us in the morning?"

Oh, brother. I knew that was coming. But why was it so hard for me to talk about my faith? Well, this was it.

"Because," I said, "that's my time to pray."

"Pray?"

"Yeah, you know, talk to God."

"You believe in God?"

"Well, I wouldn't pray to him if I didn't believe in him."

Nuts. Why did I always have to be so smart? And why couldn't I tell her that I believed in Jesus? Why was *Jesus* so hard to say? *God* is easy to say. Anybody can talk about God. *God* is so nonspecific. It says right on our American dollar bills, "In God We Trust." But it doesn't say which God. You could pick up a quarter and think, "Ah yes, in Krishna we trust." Or Buddha. Or Aphrodite. I put *my* trust in Jesus. Why didn't I say so?

"Hmmm," Gina said. "I'm glad it works for you."

Why do people always talk about Christianity as if it's a laxative? I'm glad it works for you—what's that supposed to mean? Do they mean that they tried it and it didn't work for them? Or do they mean that since I have a problem it's a good thing I have something that "works" for me?

"Hi. How ya two doin'?" Judy had slowed down to run with Gina and me.

"Fine, Judy. Just fine," I said. "I see Ed is way ahead of us." I pointed up the road. "He's probably a quarter-mile up there."

"That's okay," Judy said smugly. "He can't keep going like that forever."

I nodded. "That's true in more ways than one." It was the last thing I said for a long time. The three of us were working hard, just making it up the hill. We finally reached the top.

"That does it," Gina gasped. "I can't go on any longer."

"I'm with you," Judy said breathlessly. They both turned to me. I nodded and wheezed in agreement. Ed was nowhere to be seen.

Halfway down the hill he caught up with us.

"Hey, what's the matter? Couldn't go any farther? What a bunch of weaklings!"

"How far did *you* go?" Gina asked.

"Me? I could've kept going like that forever, but I was afraid you guys would get lost."

That was my last training run with them. While we were walking the last block to the hospital to cool down, Ed was already planning the next run.

53

"Let's meet Monday morning at seven." Ed looked at me. "Okay?" he asked. I hesitated.

"She's a Christian," Gina piped up before I could say anything. Then she lowered her voice: "She prays when she runs. That's why she likes to run alone."

Ed looked at me. "I'd pray too if I ran that slow," he snapped.

"Look," I said, "I want to *race* with you guys, but I just like to *train* alone."

My friends never asked me to run with them again. I did my training runs alone in the mornings, talking and listening to God.

It's hard for me to explain how God talks to me. It's not through lightning bolts or burning bushes. It's not as though I see his face in the test pattern on the TV. It's more of a feeling deep inside. I don't mean the kind of feeling you get dishing yourself out a second bowl of ice cream. It's more like the feeling I get after meditating on scripture, or sitting by a rushing stream, or watching a baby laugh. It's real, it's undeniable, and it floods my heart with joy.

About a week before the Bay-to-Breakers race I was out on a training run. One thing about training is that not every run is remarkable. In fact, sometimes you feel just plain awful. But that's what training is—running whether you feel like it or not. You're preparing for something yet to come. It was one of those runs. I really wanted to stay in bed. But I dragged myself out and skimmed a few chapters of the letter to the Romans in the New Testament before leaving the house.

Sometimes when I read scripture something sticks in my mind and plays over and over in my head. This time it was a sentence in the first chapter of Romans. "I am not ashamed of the gospel, because it is the power of God for the salvation of everyone who believes." As I ran, these words kept going around and around in my mind: "I'm not ashamed of the gospel. I'm not ashamed of the gospel." That's right. What I was ashamed of was myself. Why was I such a chicken? Was I afraid people would laugh? Big deal. I promised God that before that race was over I would share the good news with Gina, Ed, or Judy. I am not ashamed of the gospel. I am not ashamed of the gospel . . .

One problem with the Bay-to-Breakers race is deciding what to wear. Anybody who's ever run it knows that Bay-to-Breakers is more than a race. It's a costume party. Anything goes. In fact, even *nothing* goes. One year I was passed by a woman wearing nothing but running shoes. The year before that I ran past two people wearing gorilla suits, Santa and his reindeer, and three women dressed like honey-bees carrying a cardboard hive. You just never know.

"I think we should go as hypodermic needles," Gina said. "After all, we work in a hospital."

"Then why don't we go as bed pans?" Ed sneered.

"Flowers," said Judy. "I want to go as a garden of flowers. Little pink roses or yellow daisies—something cheerful."

"Wait. I've got it," Gina cried. "We'll go as the three blind mice and wear little spectacles and carry white canes and . . ."

"Gina, there's *four* of us," Ed reminded her.

"And—oh." She stopped. "Well, okay. What about the four musketeers?"

"That's the *three* musketeers."

"But wasn't there a movie called 'The Four Musketeers'?"

"Yeah," Judy said, "I think it was about Racquel Welch and the three musketeers."

"Great," I chimed in. "I'll go as Racquel Welch and you guys can be the three musketeers."

We ended up wearing just our ordinary shorts and T-shirts. The day started out cold and foggy, but I was prepared. I had brought some big green trash bags to wear over our clothes until we started running.

"Oh, no," Gina moaned. "Mine doesn't have any arm-holes."

"None of them come that way," I said, trying not to let her complaining bug me. She finally made armholes and a headhole like the rest of us. I looked at her carefully. "You know, Gina, maybe you should keep it on the whole race. You could go as a pickle. A big green pickle."

"I still think we should have gone as hypodermic needles," she pouted.

I turned to a kid standing next to me dressed like a caterpillar. Next to him was a little girl dressed like a butterfly. Next to her was another boy wearing a long white plastic bag stuffed with newspaper. I stared at him. "What are you supposed to be?"

"Pupa."

"What?"

"Pupa. You know, first caterpillar, then pupa, then butterfly." He pointed to the other two. "We're related."

"Yeah, I know. Larva to pupa to . . ."

"No. I mean really related. He's my brother and she's my sister."

I nodded and smiled. "Hey, that's terrific. All in the family. What does your dad do? Don't tell me—I bet he's an entymologist."

"No," the pupa said, "he writes greeting cards."

"Oh."

"Well, we're going to move up," said the caterpillar. "See you around." They wiggled and squirmed their way through the crowd, dragging their butterfly sister after them.

I turned to Judy. "Are you glad to be here?"

"I don't know yet." Judy was wearing pastel green shorts and a pastel green shirt. She looked like a walking after-dinner mint. She hadn't once asked how I was "doin'," so I knew she was nervous. I patted her on the shoulder.

"Don't worry," I said. "You can't expect to beat a caterpillar—he's got more legs than we do." She gave me a small tight grin and turned away. I sighed. Maybe now was the time. I kept thinking about my promise to God. I'm not ashamed of the gospel.

Back where we were, we never heard the starting gun. A thundering roar from the crowd signalled the beginning of the race. Then it was like sitting in a car with someone gunning the engine—lots of noise but we weren't going anywhere. Fifteen minutes passed before we actually started moving forward. Like snakes we shed our green plastic skins along with 5,000 other people. Garbage bags littered the streets like empty shrouds. Where did all the bodies go? They were moving down Howard Street, turning onto Ninth Street. Ahead lay the fabled Hayes Street Hill.

Running the road behind the Claremont Hotel had done us good. None of us had to slow to a walk up the hill. We ran past the walkers: a man in a tutu, a giant plastic snail, a couple dressed as bride and groom. We even beat the running pizza.

"How ya doin'?" Judy flashed a smile, no longer nervous.

Gina must have been hit by a surge of adrenalin at that moment. "Great! I feel wonderful. I could run forever." The three of us stared at her and shrugged our shoulders.

"I'm glad I decided to stay back and run with you guys," Ed said, jogging next to me. "It's great to hear Gina say something like that." Now it was our turn to stare at him. Judy leaned close to me.

"Boy, running in a race is really something. It has a real effect on people."

I nodded. "Yeah, but the effect is only temporary."

Judy flashed a smile. "Well, tell me what isn't."

I thought, this is it. This is my chance to tell her about God, who's not only permanent but eternal. It was the perfect moment. I would tell her how Christ could change her life forever if she'd just let him. I'm not ashamed of the gospel. I'm not. I'm not.

"Well, Judy . . ." I began as we started down the main drive in Golden Gate Park. But we ran smack into a crowd of people standing in the middle of the road.

"One-thousand-one, one-thousand-two, one-thousand-three . . ." We could hear somebody counting out the chest compressions for cardiopulmonary resuscitation. Instinctively Ed, Judy, and I broke through the crowd. A man and a woman were doing CPR on a man about fifty years old. His fat stomach lurched with each compression. His running shoes were clean and new. Ed knelt by his head.

"His pupils are fixed and dilated," he said.

There was no need to tell us. Judy and I had seen enough people who had "coded" and never made it. We knew the moment we saw him that it was too late. We heard the sound of far-off sirens, like a pack of hunting dogs coming for their prey. Ed stood up and shook his head. "Let's go."

We finished the race in silence. "I guess that's the end of that guy," Ed said as we crossed the finish line.

"Maybe not," I said. "Maybe it's just the beginning." I moved away from the others. I was frustrated and depressed. I had seen a man die and had not shared my trust in Jesus with anyone. I found a spot down a little road, away from the crowd, and dropped to my knees. Not exactly like the Garden of Gethsemane where Jesus had prayed, but it would do. I was trying to squeeze back the tears.

I will give you the right moment and the right words. Be sensitive to my Spirit.

Just then I felt a hand on my shoulder. It was Ed.

"Tough run, huh? You really maxed out, didn't you?"

I stood up. "Uh, no. I was, uh, praying." He looked at me curiously. Here at last was my chance to witness. He was obviously puzzled. Was he going to ask me about Jesus? He pointed to my legs.

"You have little rocks sticking to your knees."

"Oh. Yeah. Right. Thanks." I picked them off, wondering, did Jesus have these problems?

Still brushing dirt off my knees, I spoke. "Well you see, Ed, Jesus has really changed my life. I don't feel I have to make it all alone anymore. It was awful feeling alone—you know what I mean? Ed?"

I sighed as Ed disappeared back into the crowd. A man

in a dragon costume offered me a bottle of mineral water. I thanked him.

I looked up at the sky. "All right, God," I said, "I can wait."

Checkout

The same but different

What actually happens when you give your life to Christ?

It's not like Christians become clones of each other. If God wanted us to be exactly alike he would have created us that way. (I think he thought it would be too boring.) You actually become more "you" than ever. What if we all were covered with gallons of gross, disgusting mud? Besides not getting invited to very many parties, we would all look alike. The mud would obscure our faces and skin color and body shape. Then someone comes along and says, "I'm going to put you all in the shower." You might think we'd all come out the same, since we all are going through the same process, but actually with the mud washed from our bodies, it is apparent that we are distinct and beautiful people, not just a bunch of muddy blobs. Our different gifts become visible. The mud gets washed out of our eyes and we begin to see the beauty in other people.

It's a bit like that when we become Christians. Besides, walking around mudless is more fun!

THE POWER OF NEGATIVE THINKING

TRUE		FALSE
☐	If you don't believe exactly what I believe, you're a nerd.	☐
☐	I have complete freedom to judge other people because I'm perfect.	☐
☐	God judges me on the condition of my heart and spirit and not by how many rules I can keep.	☐

Answers at end of chapter

"Come, come, girls! Time to get up! Time to get beautiful!"

I awakened to the sound of women moaning, bathroom water running, and drawers slamming. I opened one eye in disgust. The bride had made beauty appointments for all us bridesmaids to get our hair, face, and nails done. I was still exhausted from the rehearsal the night before.

Gray is the color I hate most and I was lying on the floor with a multi-toned gray patchwork quilt thrown over me. Oh, brother.

I was annoyed by that not-quite-black-or-white excuse for a blanket and I was annoyed that Janet, the bride, thought a total stranger could know more about my hair, face, and nails than I do. I was annoyed that sleeping on a shag carpet had left furry lines like worm tracks all over my arms and thighs.

So I was lying there, a big pile of annoyance, when Janet walked in, zipping up her Calvin Kleins, and said: "Hey, we're leaving in twenty-five minutes." Her gold chains tinkled expensively against each other as she bent over and pulled the quilt off me. "Ugh, gross. You look like you've been eaten by worms."

I rolled over with a sigh, by now both eyes open in disgust. "Why don't you guys just go without me? I can do my own hair. For twenty dollars I could . . . buy eighty chocolate bars! Besides, I need some time alone."

She gave me the same look my mother used to give me when I would stay home and read a book instead of going to a dance party. "Well, suit yourself."

I sat up and reached for my running shoes. I needed to run so I could talk to Jesus about what was really annoying me. Mechanically I put on my shoes and shorts as my mind went over last night's dinner and rehearsal . . .

The rehearsal had been held in the Mission Santa Barbara. This building was a little different from your basic, everyday, run-of-the-mill church. For one thing it is really old. (The mission was one of those founded by the Catholic Spaniards who arrived several hundred years ago to "civilize" the native American Indians.) It's not the oldest, but in a state where people are obsessed with the most modern, newest, latest form of *anything*, a 200-year-old edifice is impressive.

Then of course there's the visual element. I think it's the way the pastel-colors of the wood, statues, and altar all run together. It made me feel as if I were entering an apricot-peach souffle, or maybe a religious version of a Disneyland ride. Huge oil paintings hung on either side of the altar: Mary with little golden birds flying around her head; one of Jesus crucified, bloody and gory. The wall behind the altar was filled with statues of people I supposed were saints, but I wasn't sure. One of them looked exactly like my cousin Arthur as a child and therefore ruined the heavenly effect of the whole group.

I was actually more impressed by the floor, with its large smooth stones that somebody had carefully laid down to form an even path between the pews. Every twenty feet or so a tombstone marked the life and death of someone who had given his or her life to this mission. It made me wonder if I would ever have anything to mark my life.

So we were all lined up at the altar, having "processed" down the stone aisle quite reverently, when Janet said, "Oh my gosh. I forgot. We've got to get somebody to read something out of the Bible."

They all started groaning like a high school class who had just received term paper assignments. "Oh, yuk. What are we going to do?" "Oh, brother, *I* don't want to read it—can't we skip it?"

"No, somebody has to do it. Let's get Debbie—she's religious."

Everybody looked at me and I said, "Sure, I'd love to. What's the passage?"

Janet looked momentarily confused but then her face brightened. "Oh, it doesn't matter," she said. "Pick anything you want—the book of Matthew, the book of John, something from the book of William."

The book of William? She was serious. I almost flipped out, right there at the altar of the Mission Santa Barbara. But instead I swallowed and said: "Well, I'll talk to Father Philip later and ask him what he would like." I was glad I hadn't made some sarcastic remark about the fact that there was no book of William in the Bible.

We got through the rehearsal, during which the phrase "book of William" kept running through my mind. The rehearsal dinner was green and white. Green salad, bleached chicken, overcooked broccoli, underdone rice. White wine, water, and milk. Banana ice cream for dessert.

I was waiting for Father Philip to finish all the jokes and stories he was telling. He was related to Janet's family somehow. But there was never a break in the frivolity to ask him what scripture passage I should read. After dinner I finally caught him going down the stairs. He slipped on the second step and fell into my arms, laughing. He had a bad case of hiccups.

"Father Philip! I'm glad I ran into you. I mean you ran into me. I mean . . ."

"You young girls are such jokesters! The book of William! Wasn't that cute? Now, what can I do for you?"

"I was wondering if you'd pick out some scripture reading that would be especially meaningful for Mark and Janet. I'd like to go over it tonight before I go to bed."

He looked at me as though through a haze. "Oh, heck, I dunno. I'll do it in the morning. Don't worry about it. I've done this a thousand times. Don't worry—it's not important." He turned his back and managed to make it down the stairs.

I felt as if I'd been slapped. He was a priest. But how could he be? Either he has it together or he doesn't. He should have had the scripture reading all picked out.

I stood there, ears burning, teeth clenched so tightly I almost broke my gold crown. Sweat dripped down my arms into the sleeves of my red dress. I began to get dizzy, then realized my dizziness came from not breathing. Breathing is something I forget to do when I get really angry. I suppose it's a blessing to have such an automatic shut-down system, since it prevents me from doing some things that would be totally stupid. It's pretty hard to punch somebody's lights out when you're about to faint . . .

That miserable scene kept replaying in my mind as I finished lacing my running shoes and tying back my hair. I generally like to concentrate on positive things when I run, but I could see that this morning would be different. So all these thoughts were running through my mind as *slam!* I was out the door and down the street.

I didn't know Santa Barbara at all and the only place I'd ever been to was the mission. So I set my eyes on its tower, peeking through the morning fog, and headed toward it. My body was stiff from sleeping on the floor and my mind was a casserole of negative thoughts. As I struggled up a steep grade, my breath coming in painful gulps, I started to feel a real hate for that gray quilt.

God was running beside me, but he was having no trouble with either the hill or the quilt. *It's not the quilt that's bugging you.* I don't know how Jesus manages complete sentences while running, because I never can.

Three, four, five miles went by, my body charged with the angry energy of the night before. It must have been showing on my face, because a guy at a bus stop yelled out, "Boy, I bet you'd rather be eating a hamburger!" I smiled and nodded but I was thinking that if I really had a hamburger I'd throw it at him. Still breathing in gulps, I began thinking in gulps.

Hate, hate, hate: curling hair, makeup, putting on a good face but only on the outside. Manicures, man needs cures. Filing away the rough edges, softening the skin, clipping nails, nails and snails. Go slow, slow down. Oh, God, my soul needs a manicure. File away my rough edges. Soften my heart. Maybe it's not so black and white, so "either/or." Shades of gray, perhaps? Forgive me for judging. Make me slow to anger. Forgive Father Philip.

My legs were burning with the uphill effort. I felt the anger and tension start to ooze out in my sweat and I exhaled frustration and pain. We were nearing the top of the hill. God reached out and pulled me along, because I had almost given up.

"But, I want to put on a good face from the *inside*, God. I want to feel love from the inside out. The book of William —that's tragic. Is this righteous indignation? Or is it Satan trying to get the best of me? Open my eyes, God, make me wise. Is it really a 'both/and' situation? I can both love you and disobey? People can show their love for you in ways different than mine? Sacred heart, wooden statues, smooth tiles—whoever made those things loved you as much as I do. Father Philip must love you. Let's get Debbie, Janet said. She's religious. Am I 'religious'? Am I all talk and no action? Am I like those legalistic religious leaders who were the enemies of Jesus?"

Finally we were up the hill, cruising past a rose garden, eucalyptus trees, and a group of tourists. My mind was beginning to clear. So was the sky, as the fog let go of the treetops, reluctantly—like a child leaving toys behind at bedtime. I rounded a corner and as if on cue the sun burst through the remaining fog. I finally reached the mission. Out front a kindly-looking priest was trimming the hedge. He smiled and waved. Jesus and I waved back and headed for home.

Eventually Janet and the girls returned with French braids, mauve mascara, and painted lips. By then I had showered, curled my hair, and cured my soul.

"Say, you look great," Janet said. "By the way, how did you sleep last night?"

I looked up and smiled. "Well, it would have been awful except for this," I heard myself saying. I picked up the gray quilt and folded it gently across the chair. "I have come to appreciate the shades of gray."

Answers:

1. FALSE. If you believe this to be true, in a short time you will find that **everybody** is a nerd. A statement like this is very **exclusive**. Not meaning special, but meaning that it **excludes** people. The love of God is not **ex**clusive, but **in**clusive—it **includes** everybody.

2. FALSE. "That will be the day," as my mother would say. Not only are we not perfect (yet), but we are presumptuous to assume one of God's roles—that of judge. Leave the judging to the Expert.

3. TRUE. This is the problem some of the religious leaders of Jesus' day had. If you follow a set of rules it does look good on the outside and it is much easier to fool yourself and other people. But (wouldn't you know it?), God looks in your heart and there's no fooling him. This is the difference between being "religious" and being "Christian." Being "religious" means proudly going to church, keeping commandments, and singing in the choir— all without love. Being "Christian" means letting Christ live within you and loving God, others, and yourself. There's a lot more freedom **and** responsibility in being "Christian" than in being "religious."

CHRISTMAS IN AUGUST

Has God noticed all the pain
and suffering in the world
– or is he out playing tennis
or something?

If I had seen him on the street I probably wouldn't have given him the time of day. He had long, strawberry blond hair down to the middle of his back, tied in a pony tail. Standard hippie. I can see him now, walking jauntily down the street, swinging his hands, snapping his fingers and whistling.

Of course I never really saw him like that. The last time I saw him walking down the street and whistling, he wasn't snapping his fingers. He doesn't have any fingers. In fact, he doesn't have any hands at all. He still has wavy, strawberry blond hair, but it's much shorter and it curls around his ears.

The truth is that my friendship with Barry began after his accident, after he received the 12,000 volts that burned him so badly he lost both hands and most of the flesh on his back and stomach. I wasn't sure what got into me but I thought Barry really needed someone to care about whether or not he survived, and I felt that that someone was supposed to be me. I guess I felt that way because I did his electrocardiogram the afternoon they brought him in.

When I went to the emergency department I would usually ask the front desk which room the patient was in. That time I didn't have to. I could hear him screaming. The smell of burnt flesh hit my nose the minute I walked in. I pushed my way into the trauma room through what seemed to be an endless crowd of doctors, nurses, technicians, clerks, and orderlies.

It was a hideous sight. Attached to his arms were charcoal briquets in the shape of hands. The skin on his chest and thighs was browned like something left in an oven too long.

"Oh, please. The pain. My back—the pain is so bad. Can't you just give me something that will knock me out? No. No, I'm going to be okay. I am really going to be okay."

The nurses were trying to start I.V.s. The doctor was yelling, "Let's get started on that EKG!" I was trying to put electrodes on burnt arms that couldn't feel my touch. That's when I snapped into "automatic pilot." It comes from doing hundreds of EKGs, doing them day in and day out. It doesn't mean you don't feel or notice anything. It simply means that there's an emotional time delay long enough for you to get your job done.

So it didn't matter to me that there was blood on the floor and that the EKG tracing was falling into it. It didn't bother me that there was blood all over my hands and lab coat and that the difference between the burnt stuff and his undamaged skin was literally the difference between black and white.

I finished the tracing, handed the strip to the doctor, collected the paper work at the desk, and left. I collapsed in the elevator. I went six floors up and six floors down, three times, before I could stand straight and push the EKG machine through the door. My supervisor let me go home an hour early.

I changed into my running clothes as soon as I got home. But what to pray for? A merciful death? A miraculous healing? A life of patient suffering?

As I ran along the trail under the Bay Area Rapid Transit tracks I found myself unable to talk to God. It wasn't that God wasn't listening. I simply couldn't form rational, coherent sentences in my mind. It was as if I had had my intellect removed and all that was left was emotion, raw feelings like a nerve left exposed by burned-away flesh. All I could feel was pain—deep, horrible, indignant pain.

As I ran I cried: "Oh, please, God . . ."

No lengthy explanations necessary. It's like being a child and knowing there's a monster in your bedroom. No need to call, "There's a horrible, hairy monster with purple horns and blood dripping off its teeth. Come help me!" A simple "Mom!" or "Dad!" will do. That's the kind of prayer I prayed. "Father God . . ."

The next morning at work I found out they had amputated Barry's forearms. I knew I would have to go up and see him. I had to get a different picture of him. I didn't want to carry around a memory of a blistered body screaming in the emergency room.

I went up to the burn unit, scrubbed my hands and arms, and slipped a gown over my clothes. The nurse took me down the hall.

"He's over there." He was lying very still now, so different from the last time I saw him. On either side of him were two bloody stumps, like the ends of baseball bats wrapped in yellow gauze. He was asleep, with a damp towel on his forehead. For a moment I was afraid to wake him but I saw him stir and groan.

"Barry," I called softly. "Barry?" He opened his eyes slowly. "Hi. I did your EKG down in the emergency room."

He looked confused. "You mean you're not the hooker I asked for?" My mouth dropped open. And then he started laughing, little soft ha-ha-ha's that got louder and louder and then slid into a long groan. "No, I remember you. How're you doing?"

It was my turn to look confused. He was the sick one. Why was he asking me how *I* was doing? "Well, I'm just fine."

"Good. Then would you give me some iced tea, please?"

Between sips of tea he explained how he had been painting on a scaffold with an aluminum extension pole on his roller. He was four stories up when he touched a power-line with his pole.

"Lucky I fell on the scaffold. If I had landed on those rosebushes below, that lady would have killed me." Then he broke into a crescendo of little chuckles. "But ya know, it was weird. I *felt* like I was electrocuted. My head was spinning and my body was spinning and for awhile I thought I was going to die."

The lids over his blue eyes were swollen and puffy and I could see he was having a hard time keeping them open. I reached over and adjusted the towel on his forehead. "I'll come back tomorrow and then we can talk some more."

"Okay, but don't forget the champagne and the . . ." his voice trailed off. He was asleep.

At first I could stand to spend only half an hour a day up there in the burn unit with him. I didn't know what to talk about. The smell of burned flesh and the screams of the kid in the next bed made my knees shake even when I was sitting down with a pillow over my lap to hide my trembling. But as the summer wore on I spent more and more time with him until I simply couldn't bear *not* to see him.

We talked about everything and anything: drugs, God, the Pittsburgh Steelers (he was a die-hard football fan), drugs, sex, Bing Crosby, drugs. He would always start off the conversation with some inflammatory remark to get me excited and we would go on from there.

"You know, I think there's really no God. Simply some kind of cosmic Light force, some kind of good karma going on that people just *call* God." I was incensed.

"How can you say that? If there's no God, then who created the mountains and the trees and the sunsets?"

He paused for a moment. "Proctor and Gamble. I'm sure of it. They make everything." He always had an answer. For questions, for comments, for problems, he always had an answer.

He insisted that I fed him too slowly. He wanted to do it himself. The therapist showed me how to attach a fork to his stump with a little velcro belt. He took twice as long as I did, but he didn't care. He was doing it himself.

The psychiatrist visited once or twice a week.

"He's checking to see if I've lost my marbles yet," Barry whispered to me. "He always asks me what day it is, what year it is, and who the president is." I always knew when the psychiatrist was there because I could hear Barry shouting out: "Saturday! 2001! Calvin Coolidge!" or "Wait, doc, wait. I know—Harry Truman, no, no, Jimmy Cagney, wait, wait . . ."

The boy in the bed next to him had been in the burn unit for three months already. He had been burned when a can of gasoline exploded. Physically he was doing well, but he refused to cooperate with the physical therapists and would talk only in a whiney falsetto voice. It drove Barry crazy.

"Listen, Jonathan," he yelled through the curtain one day, "you sound like a little jerk. If you want to get out of here you have to work at it. A little pain now is for a lot of good later. When I can get out of this bed I'm going to crack you on the head if you don't knock off the whining."

The entire unit fell silent. I held my breath and waited but there was no response. About twenty minutes later we heard the whoosh, whoosh, of paper slippers sliding across the floor. Jonathan appeared from behind the curtain.

"Do you want to see what my brother brought me?" he asked, producing a big picture book. He started to set the book on the bed when he noticed Barry's stumps. The book crashed to the floor.

"You'll have to pick it up yourself," Barry said matter of factly. "I'd offer you a hand but as you can see I'm a little short."

Jonathan didn't move. Barry and I burst out laughing and then slowly a smile broke across Jonathan's face. It took him ten minutes, but he picked up the book himself. After that I never heard Jonathan's falsetto whine again. He spoke in a normal voice.

I was used to Barry's sense of humor but many people were not. His insurance agent showed up one day while I was visiting.

"Hi, Barry. Came by to see you yesterday but you weren't here."

"Oh," Barry said nonchalantly, "I was getting my manicure." The agent turned red and mumbled something about coming back when Barry felt better. Barry laughed his swelling chuckle as we watched the guy disappear into the hall.

Barry turned to look at me. "I know everybody thinks I make all these jokes because I'm secretly depressed. They think that deep down inside I'm panic-stricken and that I laugh it off to cover up. I know that they're waiting for me to fall."

He was right. The nurses confided in me that they were waiting for that deep, seemingly hopeless depression that most patients go through.

"But what do I have to be depressed about?" he continued. "I still have my Adonis-like body and I'm still *alive*. You know, I should be dead. And I think one of the reasons that I'm still alive is that I took care of myself. Every morning I ran four miles around the track across from my house. And you know what? In a few months I'm going to be out there again. Of course I'll probably scare everybody off the track, but I'll be out there." He paused for a moment. "I want to start training now. Let's go for a walk."

Our walk consisted of walking fifty feet to the end of the unit and fifty feet back to his bed. We walked slowly. He stopped at the full-length mirror at the end of the hall.

"Look at me," he said flapping his arms, "I look just like a chicken."

I looked at him critically. "You're right. With that yellow gown and those skinny, chicken-white legs, you look like you just came out of an Easter basket."

He smiled. "You know why I just can't wait to use my artificial limbs?"

"No, why?"

"So I can write your phone number in all the public restrooms in Berkeley."

72

"Very funny, Chicken Little. C'mon, let's go back to your nest."

One afternoon I bounced into his room expecting the usual joke or insult but that day Barry lay quiet. His bandaged stumps were propped up on two pillows beside him. I looked into his eyes and felt his pain even before I reached his bed.

His lower lip trembled a little. "I'm not having a good day. Sorry I'm such junk. I have to go in for more surgery tomorrow—another skin graft." He turned his head away.

I couldn't speak. All I could do was stroke his head. I couldn't even hold his hand. Why, God? Why didn't you let me know him before?

He turned his head toward me. "You know what? I think God is trying to teach me something. All I used to do was paint houses so I could make money to buy dope. That's all I used to do. But I think God is showing me that there's more." That was the first time I had ever heard Barry speak about God in a positive way, or even acknowledge God's existence.

Certainly this man must believe, I said to myself. Surely he is a Christian. How could he be so cheerful and work so hard to feed himself if he didn't have God's strength? How could he talk so optimistically about his future if he didn't know that God would care for him? Even *I* didn't live so freely, and *I* was a Christian.

The second time I heard Barry mention God was in the middle of August. He had been in the burn unit for seven

---

Why is there so much pain in the world?

God doesn't send us pain or suffering to punish us. It's impossible to know for sure exactly why he allows it. What we can be sure of is that he is present with us. Because of Jesus dying on the cross, he knows exactly what it **feels** like. And he can bring good out of pain. He can also heal, physically and mentally. But these are questions which need a whole book to themselves!

weeks. In the course of our conversations we had discovered that we had both grown up on the same Bing Crosby Christmas album. So I made him a tape of "Der Bingle" and the Andrew Sisters singing "Mele Kalikimaka." I had just started the tape when he leaned over and turned up the volume with his nose.

"That's the island greeting that we send to you on this bright Hawaiian Christmas day!" The words blared out into the unit—it was like being in a department store in December. Nurses came running. Other patients wheeled their chairs to the doorway. The food service woman put down her tray. The head nurse walked into the room.

"What are you doing?"

Barry waved his stumps wildly in the air. "We're having a Christmas Party!"

"But it's the middle of August!"

"So what? Do you think that God cares *when* we celebrate the birth of his Son on earth?" He looked at me out of the corner of his eye. "Or do you think he cares what we call ourselves and what box we put ourselves in?"

The nurse scratched her head. She reached over and turned down the tape player.

"You're crazy," she said and walked out of the room—but not before she turned and glared at me.

"Mele Kalikimaka" faded out and we were left sitting in silence. He nudged me with his elbow.

"Merry Christmas." He was grinning from ear to ear.

"You're hilarious," I said sarcastically.

"Well, they can't exactly throw me out, you know. And God isn't going to throw me out. I tell you he's showing me something. He . . ." I cut him off.

"Barry, wait a minute. *I'm* the Christian. I'm supposed to be telling *you* that."

He looked at me and smiled. "You're hilarious," he said.

The last time we talked about God was in a letter that I wrote to Barry thanking him for being such a wonderful friend and courageous guy, for cheering *me* up all the time when I was supposed to be cheering him up. I told him that I loved him and would always pray for him and maybe could he come to church with me one Sunday?

He wrote back a postcard on which he had scrawled the words, "You're hilarious. Love, Barry." That's all.

How can a person be so good and not be a Christian?

It is useless for us to try to divide the world up into Christians and non-Christians. For one thing, it's impossible to know for sure. For another, everybody is presently on a "journey."

There are people who call themselves "Christian" whose lives slowly make it clear that they aren't Christians at all. Some are becoming Christian. Others don't completely agree with all Christian doctrine but are so attracted to Jesus that they may be more "his" than they know.

Of course it makes life easier when we label people—then we don't have to consider each person as a unique individual, and we don't have to give them any credit for the journey they're on.

Categorizing people is convenient . . . but it's also lazy and narrow-minded. At the end of the journey, God won't be asking us about other people, but about where **we** stand in relation to him.

JUST A FAT KID

Is it possible to get rid of an unwanted grudge?

What about unwanted pudge?

When depressed, bored, or lonely, do you eat ice cream with hot fudge?

The smell of cedar hung in the air. Flickering light from the fire danced off the pine rafters. We had made our escape. The pressure, pollution, and noise of the city were far behind us. I sighed contentedly on the couch in our refuge—a small mountain cabin. Brian stroked my head as it lay in his lap. His other hand was locked with mine. We were staring dreamily into the fire. I looked up at him.

"Brian, don't you think the flames look like—like golden red salamanders dancing in the fire?"

"Mm. Mm-hmm . . ."

I smiled to myself. "Brian," I reached up and touched his face, "what are you thinking?"

He looked down at me and sighed. "Well, I was thinking that if you put a hood over that fireplace it would draft a lot better. Why? What are you thinking about?"

"Murder. Maim and mutilation."

"Huh?"

"Never mind." I sat up. Straightening my hair, I said, "I can't believe how your mind works! I never know what kind of mood you're in or if anything is bugging you. You always know what's bugging me because I tell you right away."

"That's for sure."

I poked him in the stomach. "No, really. You have to tell me things. C'mon, tell me what bugs you about me."

"Well, I don't know. Gee, uh—nothing. Well . . . okay. It bugs me that you don't like to drive. I mean, what's the big deal with driving? You always complain about it."

I grinned. This was going to be easier than I thought. "Okay, you're right. I shouldn't complain about driving. I'm just lazy. What else?"

"I don't like it when you get in one of your wacky moods and make jokes non-stop and nobody can talk to you seriously."

I nodded. "You're right. It's totally childish and immature. I'm insensitive to other people's feelings. What else?"

He hesitated and looked closely at me. "Um . . . well, this next thing I say with fear and trembling."

I felt a giggle rising up out of me. I bet he was going to say that he hated my glasses.

"I don't like your—well, your eating habits. I saw you eat ten chocolate chip cookies in a row! And I know for a fact that you've polished off a one-pound box of gourmet chocolates in one day. You know, if you lost ten pounds you could be an incredibly attractive woman."

Gloom closed in around me. My heart skipped at least one beat. My throat did a couple of gulps. No telling how many knots my stomach tied itself into. In a state of psychological paralysis, I sat rigidly, comtemplating doom.

"Really, Deb, you always make jokes about your thighs being fat, but you never do anything about it. And you give *me* a bad time about not running. Well, I don't eat half the junk you do."

Gloom and doom? That room was a tomb—you could say I died right then and there. I've always thought of my ego as being a separate part of me, larger and more fragile than my spiritual self. There was my ego—hacked up with a meat cleaver and strewn around the cabin. Tears trickled down my face and suddenly I was that fat ten-year-old kid again. My dad with his arm around me was saying, "Well, I don't know, honey. Maybe if you lost some weight you'd have more friends." I turned away from Brian and swallowed.

"Yeah. I guess you're right. I ... I ... eat too much . . ." I couldn't talk because of the sob that was choking me. I couldn't look at Brian because anybody except Miss Universe who has ever tried to talk while crying knows that you end up speaking in grunts, your mouth gets contorted, and you look like a rabid dog about to bite.

Brian reached over to wipe the tears off my face. "Please," he said. "Please, I didn't mean to make you cry."

I shook my head and smiled. "Hey, no big deal. It's all right. After all—I asked for it. It's late. Think I'll turn in. Goodnight." He reached out to pull me back down on the couch but I moved away. "See you in the morning!" I said cheerfully.

I crept quietly up the stairs into the loft, trying not to wake Laurie in the next bed. I slid thankfully under the sheet and pulled the quilt over my head. I wished I could stay under there forever. I could hear an occasional cricket chirp and the wind making midnight rounds through the trees. It was a warm night so Laurie had opened the window but I lay there shivering. When sleep finally came it was filled with vivid and horrifying dreams.

I was sitting at a big table stuffing my face. I was surrounded by cream-oozing cakes, soft-center chocolates, cheese-flavored tortilla chips, triple hamburgers, and lemon meringue pies. My thighs were growing huger by the minute, like balloons being filled from a helium tank. Brian was down at the other end of the table trying to shout something at me, but I couldn't hear him. I grabbed my fork and was about to stab a marzipan cherry. The fork slipped out of my hand and fell tines-down onto my thigh. Bam! I popped open. The noise of the explosion was indescribable and, just like a pinata, millions of little wrapped candies came spilling out of me onto the floor.

"I tried to tell you!" Brian was waving his arms and

shouting. I looked down at my punctured thigh. I would never run again!

I woke up in a cold sweat, my throat tight from sobbing. I went downstairs, took some bicarbonate, and returned to bed. This time I dreamed I was sleeping between the two chocolate wafers of a cream-filled cookie. I woke up groaning, "Get this icing off me!" as I shoved the quilt off the bed. I sat up jerkily, breathing hard as if I had just sprinted a lap around the track.

I looked around. The bed resembled a re-enactment of the Civil War. The pillows were halfway across the room and I had knocked over my little travel alarm. I looked in the mirror. I looked like somebody who had *fought* in the Civil War. I could hear the others downstairs making breakfast. How could I face them? Me and my thighs? I felt awful. I grabbed for my running shorts. Pray, that's it. That's what I have to do. God will fix it. I'll just take a run with him and I'll be fine in no time. I got dressed and hurried downstairs.

"Good morning!" everyone called brightly. I smiled briefly at Bill and Laurie but ignored Brian.

"Hi. Don't wait for me. I have to go run."

Laurie looked concerned. "Well, how long will you be gone?"

"Not long." I slammed the door behind me, leaving Brian with a bewildered look on his face.

Soon I was flying down the mountain trails, pine needles crunching under my feet and the brisk morning air numbing my ears.

"Well, God," I said, "what am I going to do? I feel so awful. I want Brian to love me for myself, not for how I look."

Usually when I run I take some time to hear what God is saying, and I come back from a run renewed in spirit and full of energy. Looking back, I can see what happened that morning. I couldn't hear what God was trying to tell me because I was so busy feeling sorry for myself—and making battle plans.

How could Brian be so insensitive? All my life I've been

just a fat kid with no friends. It's taken me months and months to believe that people love me for who I am and not what I look like, and he's just undone all that work in two minutes!

I looked down at my thighs. Ugh! They're fat. They were rubbing together. I ran down a path that opened into a street and past some small cabins. A man and his wife were out front raking up pine needles. They stared at me as I ran by. He said something to his wife that I couldn't hear, but I knew what he said. He turned to her in amazement and said: "Gee, Marge, did you see those thighs? Looked like those hams we had at Christmas. Ain't that somethin'!"

I ran hard up the hill beyond that cabin, tears stinging my eyes. "God? Where are you? What do you have to say to this?" You'd think God would come in loud and clear at 8,000 feet elevation, but I didn't hear a thing.

"Well," I said aloud, "I'll show Brian. I'll lose weight and get gorgeous and then millions of guys will be dating me and he'll say, 'I want you, now,' and I'll say, 'Get lost, turkey.' Hah!"

I returned to the cabin with a smug smile on my face. Everyone looked up when I came in.

"Feeling better?" Laurie asked.

"Oh, sure," I answered in a sinister voice. "Much better."

That day we decided to take a short trip to explore an old mining town. It was cute and quaint and filled with corny exhibits and expensive little shops. We passed an exhibit of how they used to slaughter pigs and cure the pork. They had big plastic pigs hanging from the ceiling on hooks.

I sidled up to Brian. "Why are you staring? See someone you know?"

He sighed and began to say something, but I had disappeared into the county jail.

"Hey, let me take a picture of you guys in front of the county jail," Bill said, whipping out his camera. He started focusing. "Come on, Brian, stand closer to Deb.

Okay, great, great. That's super. Now smile. Stand up straight."

"And suck in your thighs," I muttered under my breath. The picture came out with me smiling and Brian looking like I had just stabbed him. He finally cornered me by the mannequin of a blacksmith beating on a plaster anvil.

"Listen, I'm sorry for what I said last night. I didn't mean to hurt your feelings. I didn't realize you were sensitive about your weight."

I flinched when he said weight. "It's all right. I forgive you." My fingernails were digging into the plaster anvil and leaving white marks like some kind of bizarre animal tracks. "I guess I just can't get it out of my mind. But it's okay. Really."

The day was hot and the western street dry and dusty. We stopped at the corner saloon to "wet our whistles" as Laurie suggested.

"Okay, drinks are on me." Brian pulled out his wallet. "What'll you have?" He looked at the three of us.

"Sasparilla, pardner."

"Ginger ale."

"Soda water," I said with just a trace of sarcasm in my voice.

After Laurie realized that she had been short-changed in The Old-Fashioned Candy Shoppe, and Bill had stepped in a pile of horse poop, we decided to leave.

On the way back to the cabin Brian wanted to stop at a discount store and check out crock pots. "C'mon," he coaxed, "come in and look at them with me." I went reluctantly and we left Laurie and Bill in the car.

"Ah, here they are," Brian said triumphantly. He put his arm around me. "Now which one would you choose?"

I felt the horns popping up on my head. "The *biggest* one. So I could make *lots* and eat it *all*." He took me by the shoulders and turned me around to face him.

"Just when are you going to get over this?" The anger in his voice was like a slap across the face.

"Give me some time," I said evenly.

We were too tired that night to make popcorn or sing

songs or any of those other fun things you're supposed to do when you're up in the mountains. Brian went to bed without saying goodnight. Bill followed soon after, and then Laurie, promising to leave the night light on for me.

"No, please don't bother. It's okay. I can find my bed." She nodded and went upstairs. So there I sat, all alone in front of the fireplace staring this time into burning embers instead of leaping flames. I felt heavy. No, not just my body, but in my soul. My heart was leaden and I wanted to cry. But my eyes were like hard metal and there were no tears there. There were no crickets that night. I could hear only the cabin creaking sympathetically to me.

How many times should I forgive my brother? Seventy times seven, it says in the Bible, and while I couldn't do the math in my head, I realized it meant I should forgive my brother or my sister *every* time.

"Oh, God," I whispered, "I'm such a jerk. Forgive." I drew my knees up to my chest and hugged them tightly against me. "Please forgive me."

Of course I forgive you. Now it's your turn.

I once read that God loved in proportion as he forgave, and suddenly I felt a surge of love for Brian in proportion to how much I must forgive and forget. I put my head down and started to cry. Now, if only Brian would forgive *me*.

They don't call God the Master Planner for nothing. Just then Brian's door opened. He walked slowly across the room and sat down beside me.

"Brian, I'm such a jerk . . ."

"No, *I* am. I do love you for who you are. I . . ."

"No, you're right. I'm a pig with the eating habits of a juvenile delinquent! I lust after Three Musketeers—not the men—the candy bar!"

He clapped his hand over my mouth. I tore it away. "No, no, not your hand! I'll eat that too!"

"But you won't eat this!" He grabbed a pillow off the couch and held it against my mouth until I quit squirming and shrieking. Then he set it down on the floor and took my hands in his. We sat there for a long time staring into the fading coals—Brian holding my hands and me thanking God for his mercy but still feeling that my jeans were too tight.

Finally Brian moved. "Hey," he said ruffling my hair, "what are you thinking?"

"Well," I said softly, "I was thinking that if you put a hood over your face you'd have more friends. What are you thinking?" I didn't hear what he said because I fell into a convulsing heap of laughter. He waited until I calmed down to just coughing and wiping the tears from my eyes.

"Patience," he said through clenched teeth. "I'm thinking about God teaching me to be patient."

"You're right," I said. "What else?"

He looked at me out of the corner of his eye. "I'm hungry."

I frowned. "Hmmm. Popcorn?"

"Definitely."

"Butter?"

"Of course."

I hesitated. "It's 152 calories per cup."

"Who cares?"

"Right."

Brian threw another log on the fire and we laughed, all three of us. God seems to enjoy buttered popcorn. But of course he doesn't have to worry about calories.

Checkout

And you thought the "Fudge Factor" was a scientific term . . .

Aspirin is the most commonly recommended medicine, but I bet more people eat chocolate to relieve their discomforts. If food consumption has become a major source of problems for you, ask yourself these questions:

Time: When do I eat? □ 2 a.m. □ all the time □ almost never
Mood: What am I feeling like? □ bored □ angry □ depressed □ happy
Location: Where do I eat? □ at the table □ watching TV □ in bed □ on the way to work or school?
Quantity: How much do I eat? □ enough to feed an army □ a flea □ a normal human of my size?
Quality: What do I eat? □ a good balance of protein, carbohydrates, and fats □ mostly junk food □ anything I can get my hands on

If you find yourself always eating or **not** eating because you're bored, lonely, or depressed, your food intake is a symptom of a bigger problem. Understanding **why** you're unhappy and what you can do about it is the first step.

IS THERE LIFE AFTER
THE DEATH OF A ROMANCE?

> Do broken hearts heal faster
> in a plaster cast, a cardiac care unit,
> or a bowl of chicken soup?

> Was my eight-year-old
> best friend right when she said,
> "Boys are icky"?

I've always loved Christmas carols. My family has had Christmas records for as long as I can remember. When I was a little girl I liked to sit with my ear right on the speaker and sing along in a loud voice. I knew them all by heart and I took each one very seriously. I can remember walking down the dark hall into my parents' bedroom and saying gravely: "With my eyes aglow, I find it hard to sleep tonight. I know that Santa's on his way. He's bringing lots of toys and goodies on his sleigh. And—" My mom and dad marched me back to bed with a warning that I'd better not cry and I'd better not pout because Santa Claus really *was* coming to town and he didn't like kids who couldn't sleep.

The songs I couldn't relate to as an adolescent were the ones that talked about snow (in California we never had any) and the mushy ones about love (because I never had a boyfriend around Christmas).

Now I was grown up, though, and this was going to be a big year for me: for the first time I would have someone to kiss under the mistletoe, roast chestnuts with over an open fire, and walk with in a winter wonderland.

At last my December holidays would look like those on the Doris Day Christmas album: exchanging gifts with a handsome man in front of a roaring fire, holding hands during the Christmas Eve church service. So I put up mistletoe, cleaned out the fireplace, and bought chestnuts.

About a week after I bought those chestnuts, Brian and I decided to go over to San Francisco to shop and check out the Christmas window displays. We started out early that Saturday morning with a cappucino at a Berkeley café. We sat outside on the café deck, blinking in the early morning sun and warming our hands around our coffee cups. The streets were still empty, quiet, and fresh.

Most of Berkeley was still asleep in their water beds, orthopedic posture-perfect beds, and goose-down sleeping bags. I smiled to myself and thought, if they only knew the joy of being up early and having a whole Saturday ahead of them. It's like that first bite of a candy bar, when you just want to savor the moment because you know you still have a whole bar ahead of you. It's delicious. We had a whole day ahead of us. Maybe Brian would take my picture with Santa Claus. Or maybe it would rain really hard and we could sit in a nice warm restaurant and watch it come down. Or the thick bay fog might come rolling in and be almost like snow and there would be Christmas bells and . . .

"Are you done?" Brian's question cut short my fantasies.

"Sure. The coffee was great. Let's go." It was as if I had never been to the city before. Driving across the Bay Bridge I had to roll down the window and stick out my head.

"Wow! Can you believe it?" I shouted, the wind blowing the words out of my mouth. "It's like a postcard. Everything is so clear. The Pyramid building looks like cut glass."

I pulled down the sun visor and looked at myself in the mirror. Sticking my head out the window hadn't been a good idea—I now looked more like a Christmas manger animal than Doris Day. By the time I got all the knots combed out of my hair we had found a parking place at

Ghiradelli Square. I don't know why I like that place so much. It doesn't have as many shops as some other places, but it's old and has a lot more character. Or maybe it's because they make terrific chocolate there. It's sort of a Bethlehem for chocolate lovers.

I think we were still in Ghiradelli when things between us started to get weird. After lots of window shopping we went into a charity bazaar to pick out a pair of knitted mouse-slippers for my sister. You know the kind—sort of like socks, with knitted ears, nose, and tail and those plastic wiggly eyes. They do look pretty much like mice, except for the eyes. If you ever saw a real mouse with eyes like that and caught it and turned it over to the proper authorities you'd probably get some kind of prize. But the eyes look cute on knitted slippers. I told Brian I definitely preferred the brown slippers because they looked more realistic.

"Nobody is going to think she's wearing real skinned mice on her feet anyway," he argued. "So why do you care if they're more realistic? Get the black ones with the red ears. They're more impressive."

"Those look stupid," I snorted. "Like they put his ears in a blender. I'm getting the brown ones." I was starting to get a headache. How could I be tired already? Or maybe I was getting hungry. We had nibbled Ghiradelli chocolate for lunch.

Then just as we were leaving the square, around the corner behind us came a pack of kids on skateboards. There were at least eight or nine of them, screaming and yelling and careening around shoppers like the silver shots in a pinball machine. Up ahead were two women around sixty, both wearing navy blue raincoats which I suspect they wore to make them look thinner. They also had identical pairs of navy shoes, the kind with a little stacked heel that is supposed to be comfortable for walking—but not if your feet are stuffed into them like theirs were.

The two women stopped ambling along to gaze at a long-tailed kite flying above them. Their stop was a little too sudden. One of the kids came crashing down behind the woman who had pointed to the kite, his skateboard colliding with the back of her heel. She gave a yelp that sounded like my mom's chihuahua getting its nails cut. I started to laugh, but the chuckle died in my throat as I saw blood pouring down the back of her shoe. The kids were gone before she could even turn around.

"You little brats! You no-good-for-nothings! I could kill you! I could *kill* you!" She limped over to a bench, sat down, and dabbed at her foot with a Kleenex.

Brian and I had witnessed the whole thing. Behind us in the square, Christmas music was blaring out:

> *Children laughing, people passing,*
> *Meeting smile after smile,*
> *And on every street corner you hear. . .*

"Screaming," I filled in. "You hear screaming." I felt awful. I must be hungry. I turned to Brian. "Let's go have an early dinner."

So at 4:30 we were the first ones at the restaurant door in North Beach. Waiters were still setting up tables when we were seated in the front window. My spirits began to pick up. Now we would have time just to sit and talk. Veal piccata, a little red wine, sourdough French bread.

I reached over and took Brian's hand. "I really like you a lot." Brian had a phobia about the word *love* so I was always careful not to say it even though I had loved him for a long time. He once told me he would never tell a woman he loved her unless he was going to propose marriage. For months now he had been telling me how much he "liked" me. But that was okay with me. I knew he would see the light soon—maybe while roasting chestnuts—and until then I didn't need him to love me back.

"Well, that's what I want to talk to you about," he said putting down his fork. The colored lights were blinking on-off against the tinsel in the window.

Wishing you a merry little Christmas,
May your hearts be light,
From now on your troubles will be
out of sight . . .

"You know, we spend a lot of time together," he began.

"Uh huh."

"And, well, the truth is, I just don't know how I feel. I think we should start seeing each other maybe only once a week."

A piece of veal fell off my fork.

"Well, Deb, how do *you* feel?"

How do I feel? I feel like I'm at the dentist and he's just told me that they all have to come out. How does he *think* I feel? "Well, I don't feel like I just won the Irish Sweepstakes," I said.

"No, c'mon. How do you feel?"

"I don't feel like talking about it right now." The tinsel was blurring and I concentrated on the blinking lights to keep my tears from spilling over. Suddenly my veal piccata looked like dog food. "Excuse me, could I have this wrapped up to take home?" I asked the waiter.

Brian looked at me. "Are you full already?"

No, I'm totally nauseated, I thought to myself. But I just grinned weakly and said, "Yes, I guess I ate too much chocolate today."

After dinner we walked up to Coit Tower. The climb was interminable, cold and dark. I felt as if I were being led to the gas chamber. When we finally got to the top I looked around at the city lights and then realized we were surrounded by kissing couples. I choked at the sight of them. At least it was dark—I never look good when I cry. I know some people who are downright appealing with tears streaming down their faces, dropping into their laps or onto their pretty little hands. My tears always go down the sides of my nose and drip straight into my mouth. My eyelids swell, my cheeks get blotchy, and my mascara smears under my eyes and looks like that black stuff the football players wear.

I pulled myself together and we walked over to a nearby eucalyptus grove. I stepped up on a stump so I could look into Brian's face. I took a deep breath.

"Okay, I'll tell you how I feel. I think it's great that you don't throw the word *love* around all the time. I respect you for sticking to what you believe. But I, but . . ." Oh, no, I was beginning to lose it. A hard-boiled egg had mysteriously formed in my throat. I swallowed it down. ". . . but I think you're a fool. Why are you so afraid of love? Why are you so afraid of commitment? I'm not talking marriage—I just want you to love me." That was the last coherent thing I said.

Brian put his arms around me and I stood there shaking and sobbing on his shoulder just like in the movies. But unlike the movies I was wondering if I was getting his jacket all gross, and why didn't I bring a nice hanky? (Because I don't own one, that's why.)

The drive home across the bridge was deathly quiet. Brian looked straight ahead and I looked out the window. The calm before the storm. We pulled up to my house, and Brian turned off the lights and shut off the engine. I looked up through the windshield, past the power lines and TV antennas. The night was still clear and the stars seemed brighter than I'd ever seen them.

> *Oh holy night, the stars are brightly shining—*
> *It is the night of our dear Savior's birth.*
> *Long lay the world, in sin and error pining . . .*

Well, I wasn't in error, and I refuse to pine for anybody. "Well, Brian, what do you want to do?" I asked evenly.

He paused. "I don't know. I—I feel pressure. I don't want to start resenting you. I—I need a break."

"All right," I snapped. "I'll make it easy for you. Let's break up. Don't call me, don't come over, don't ask my friends about me." I picked up my mouse slippers and veal piccata. I leaned over and kissed him. "Thanks for a great day. I love you. Goodbye."

Looking back, I don't know how I managed to get through that first week. I followed my usual prescription

92

for depression: I ran a lot, slept a lot, and drank a lot of water. I was worried about Brian, though, so I called his brother in Pennsylvania and told him what happened. I asked him to call Brian and make sure he was okay. I called my sister in Hawaii for sympathy and said brave things like, "If this is God's will, then it's all right with me. I think he is teaching me to lean on him and not Brian. But oh, Lynie, what shall I do?"

I listened to Christmas records constantly that week, but only the instrumental ones—I couldn't bear to hear the words.

> *Later on we'll conspire, as we dream by the fire,*
> *To face unafraid, the plans that we made—*
> *Walking in a winter wonderland.*

Finally, after a week, I called my friend Hammersly who lived in Davis. She listened sympathetically and then I began my Brave Woman spiel. "I think I'm learning to lean on God instead of . . ." She cut me off.

"So why are you calling me? I mean, if you're leaning on God, you should feel some peace about this. Have you really prayed about it?"

I was shocked into silence. *Had* I prayed about it? Maybe, if you count walking around moaning "Oh, God" as praying. We talked a little more and then I hung up feeling empty and frustrated.

It was only 10 a.m. but I had already clocked twelve hours of sleep and drunk four glasses of water. I got dressed to run. The last few days I had been feeling weak as I ran. Maybe this morning would be better. As usual, though, the first mile was almost enough to make me hang up my running shoes forever. Then I started to feel better. Mechanically I began to pray, "God, if this is your will, then that's fine with me—if Brian and I aren't supposed to be together . . ." Then I started thinking about Brian and wondering how he was feeling. Did he even think about me once all week? I thought of how our friendship had grown so slowly, carefully, and cautiously into something more, something deeper.

I was getting a stitch in my side now but I welcomed it. I wanted to see if I could hurt as much physically as I did emotionally. I thought about all the times we had prayed together, and then I thought about the mistletoe and the chestnuts and the fire—for the first time in my life there would have been someone special at Christmas time. I closed my eyes and saw the Doris Day album. The stitch was worse, so I started panting to ease the pain. But I couldn't ease the pain in my heart. Everything had been perfect until God got into it. Who asked him anyway? Dreams by the fire. Winter wonderland. My panting turned to sobbing and I looked up at the gray sky.

"All right!" I yelled. "I surrender! I'm yours. Do what you want with me, God."

Why are you so afraid of commitment? I just want you to love me.

Those words sounded familiar. I thought about Jesus. Did he know what it felt like to be rejected?

Sweet little Jesus boy, they made you be born in a manger,
Sweet little holy child, we didn't know who you were—
Didn't know you came to save us Lord,
To take our sins away—
Our eyes were blind, they could not see—
We didn't know who you were.

Of course Jesus knows! Oh Lord, I thought, how did you keep going? Did you feel like your heart was breaking? Was it knowing that God your Father loved you and had a special purpose for you on earth that kept you going?

Of course. The answer couldn't have been more obvious. It could have been more subtle, but not to me; God has to jump up and down and yell in my ear before *I* get the message. That's why Jesus came down here and stayed for thirty-three years—so he could experience every single misery, rejection, and temptation that anyone would come across. He even started out as a poor baby born in a manger.

The stitch in my side was gone now and I was starting to feel stronger, my breathing more even. Yes, God. Bend me, break me, make me yours. I know you love me and have a special purpose for me, too. I surrender. I'm yours.

It was as if I had been holding my breath all my life and finally let it go and relaxed and was still. I turned the corner and headed for home. I was free.

Hammersly was down from Davis for the weekend. That afternoon we went to buy our Christmas trees at the lot where Brian was working. I didn't have to act anymore. God was taking care of me. Brian bounded out from behind some fir trees, with chain saw in hand. Oh no, I thought, he's still mad. But he laid the saw down on the ground and walked over to us. I had to catch my breath. I was so glad just to see him. He looked better than ever, even though his hands were black with sap and little green needles were sticking everywhere out of his sweater. We stood there, just looking at each other.

"Look at this," Brian said, grabbing a bushy pine. "Best one in the lot. It's excellent. And for $23.50 it's a deal."

Hammersly loved it immediately. "That's the one I picked out first. It's perfect. Let's get it." But I wasn't so sure. Besides, if we bought it and left I wouldn't get a chance to talk to Brian.

"Well, I don't know," I said. "I think we better look around." I turned and walked down a row of fir trees. Hammersly shrugged and went another way.

Brian followed me. "How are you doing?"

"Me? Ha-ha, of course you mean me. I don't suppose you've started talking to the trees now, have you? Well, I'm doing much better." Then I just sort of nodded my head and smiled, because I felt myself start to cry.

Somebody put an arm around me. It was Jesus. *I didn't say it would be easy, just that I will hold you up.*

I straightened up and walked back over to the first tree, Brian tagging along behind. "I think we'll take this one after all." Brian helped us tie the tree on the car and in no time we were heading back home.

"You did very well," Hammersly said. "I'm proud of you."

"Thanks," I said. I looked at my watch. "We'd better get going. It's getting late and I still have to make garlic bread for that dinner."

So there I was, peeling and crushing garlic, when the doorbell rang. Hammersly was talking on the phone.

"I'll get it," I called, and went to the door, garlic in one hand, dishtowel in the other. It was Brian. I bet he didn't charge us enough for the tree, I thought.

"Hi. Can I talk to you for a minute?"

"Sure," I said, not moving.

"Do you mind if I come inside?"

"Oh. Of course not. Come in."

He looked over at Hammersly on the phone.

"Um, well, let's go upstairs," I said. We sat on the edge of the bed. Brian cleared his throat. I was still clutching my dishtowel.

"I've come to a realization," he said.

And you're moving back to Pennsylvania because you can't stand the sight of me, I thought.

"I've come to the realization that I—that I really love you." He could have told me he had a shotgun in his jacket and was planning to blow my brains out, and I couldn't have been more surprised. It was the moment I had been waiting for, but there were no chestnuts, no fire, and no silver bells. It was what I had abandoned any hope of when I surrendered to God. I couldn't believe it. I just sat there picking garlic out of my fingernails. I didn't know what to say. What would Doris Day do?

I finally looked up. "I love you too."

"Good," he said.

We didn't fly into each other's arms like they do in those Gothic novels. Brian quietly took my hand and we sat very still, not talking. My heart had been bruised and was not quite healed yet. I was reluctant to hand it out again so quickly. Better to heal in God's time.

Brian took a deep breath and squeezed my hand. "There's something else. I've been offered a great job— back in Pennsylvania."

"Are you going to take it?"

Checkout

Common myths about love

Myth 1: Love means never having to say I'm sorry.
Truth: Love not only means having to say "I'm sorry," but "I'm wrong," "I forgive you," and "I love you."

Myth 2: Love is blind.
Truth: Love is **not** blind—on the contrary, love has **vision**. Love sees the good in people and accepts the not-so-good. Love has x-ray eyes which see through anger, fear, and rejection and heal a hurting person.

Myth 3: If I love someone—I should marry them.
Truth: Think of all the men/women you know and love—could you see yourself married to all of them? **Any** of them? And do you know the difference between love and infatuation? Is love enough to insure a happy marriage?
 Love is, indeed, an important factor, but it's also necessary to consider your life goals, common interests, and spiritual lives. Putting your faith in God and then being able to share that faith is crucial to your personal growth. In a way, God is selfish—he wants us to be completely his. He wants us to put him first. And then the details of life—where to go and what to do—will begin to be made clearer to us.

"Yes. I can't pass it up. It would be great experience. . ." His voice trailed off.

I looked up at him.

"Take it. I think it's wonderful. We'll always be friends."

Brian looked surprised. But he didn't know that I had really surrendered and was finally free. My self-worth was not based on Brian's loving me or on my having him. My happiness depended on letting Brian go and following God.

He leaned over and put his arms around me. "Thanks Deb."

I reached up to touch his face but he grabbed my hand mid-way. "Ugh, what's that smell?"

"That's just Jack Frost nipping at your nose," I answered.

> *Silent night, holy night,*
> *All is calm, all is bright . . .*

FOREVER

Definition of forever:

Something that lasts until you die.

Diamonds

The time spent fixing your hair in the morning.

Something that lasts even **after** you die.

Joy is the only adult friend I have who is shorter than I am. She has a low voice, a soft deep laugh, and yards and yards of thick Japanese hair that falls in waves over her shoulders. She's been a special friend ever since we first met at camp.

We were working in a Christian summer camp with a bunch of kids we called the "Demonic Half-wits." You know the kind: they put full-strength cologne in their squirt guns, throw you in the lake, and stuff squidgy cake in the bottom of your sleeping bag. Joy and I memorized Romans chapter 5, verses 3 and 4 that week. We would walk around repeating under our breath: "Suffering produces perseverance, perseverance character and character hope." Pretty soon we had it down to just initials: S.P.C.H. After cleaning up a lap-full of creamed corn to the accompaniment of shrieks and giggles, Joy leaned over to me and said: "We'll just have to call the S.P.C.H." So our relationship was first built on raw need, then on growing love and mutual understanding. Much the same as getting to know someone in a foxhole during an attack.

In the two years since camp we had seen each other maybe only a dozen times. But our relationship was special. We were the kind of friends who can see each other rarely yet still not lose ground. We never felt we had to make up for lost time—we simply picked up where we left off. So when she called me from Phoenix one night in August to tell me she was getting married and to ask if I would be in her wedding, I was honored and delighted but not surprised.

I was giving myself a mud facial the night she called.

"Hello, Deb?"

"Joy! Hi, how are you?" I said through clenched teeth.

"Am I calling at a bad time?" she said cautiously. "You sound a little tense."

"No, no," I mumbled. "I just put a mud pack on my face. I might as well let it dry. Tell me what's new and exciting."

"Oh, well, okay," her voice brightened. "My job is working out really well. I love being a physical therapist."

"Uh-huh."

"Mom and Dad are doing great. The heat out here is terrible, of course, so I spend all my spare time floating in the pool. My brother Steve is going to summer school."

"Uh-huh, uh-huh." I could feel the mud getting tighter on my face.

"And I just talked to Terry tonight in Colorado. She is really frustrated in her job. It was amazing—we talked for two hours!"

"No kidding." I picked up a hand mirror and held it up to my face. I looked like one of those Greek drama masks —the tragic one. My face was totally immobile, as though it was encased in a plaster cast.

She paused and I could hear her take a deep breath. Her usual low soft laugh was now high-pitched. "And—well, Gary and I are getting married!"

"What?" I screamed into the phone. Intense pain. "Ay-y-h-h, my face! I think I broke it." I was no longer a human being but a shattered plate glass window. Little bits of dried mud were falling onto my desk. "Joy, hold on. I'll be right back. I ran into the bathroom, filled the sink with water, and dunked my head. Relief. Pieces of mud still clung to my nose when I got back to the phone.

"Joy, I'm really sorry. About leaving the phone, that is. You're getting married! That's great. I'm really happy for you."

"Are you going to be busy in January?" she asked.

"Me? Busy in January? Well of course there will be Aspen for two weeks' practice on the slopes and then off to Zurich for some *real* skiing. But that's only after I celebrate New Year's Eve with Robert Redford."

"I want you to be in our wedding."

"In your wedding? I'd love to! I'm sick of Switzerland anyway and I can be with Robert at Christmas."

I was getting all choked up thinking about the wedding and suddenly realized that a few chunks of clay mask had fallen down inside my typewriter.

"We hung up after forty-five more minutes of the proposal description, cake controversy, and the marvel of how God had managed to find just the right man for her.

January finally came. California was being besieged by storms and floods, so when I got off the plane in Arizona I sensed that I was stepping out into a foreign country or even a different planet. Joy's brother Dave picked me up at the airport.

Dave and I are just as close as I am to Joy. It may be the simple fact that we've known each other longer, or it may be because Dave and I operate on the same plane. We first met when he was youth minister at Berkeley Covenant Church: I liked him the moment I met him. I never had to go into detailed explanations about how I was feeling. He never had dumb ideas about things. And he loved good coffee and scented candles. That's what I mean by our being on the same plane.

Dave also likes to run. On the rare occasions when I didn't run alone, I ran with Dave. We ran the streets of Berkeley, carefully dodging speeding cars, dog desserts, and Hare Krishnas. Our favorite time was any clear morning when the sun was still yawning and stretching its way up into the sky and the air was ginger-snap cool. We would run across the Berkeley campus, through the eucalyptus grove (where I was always haunted by child-hood memories of Vick's Vapo-Rub), then by the campus coffee house where even on Saturday we could see students clutching cups of cappucino and staring at their books. I did not envy them, with their eyeballs looking like peeled tomatoes. Their under-eye bags seemed to deepen exponentially as the end of each quarter drew near. I felt such freedom, being on campus but not as a student.

We would continue running, across the bridge, over Strawberry Creek, and past the life sciences building. Occasionally we said good morning to a befuddled street person just crawling out of his sleeping bag in the juniper bushes. We jogged by ecology-conscious citizens sorting out their bottles and cans, and passed high school students with huge transistor radios hermetically sealed to their ears. We courageously ran down Telegraph Avenue, without so much as a penny for the street people asking everyone, "Spare change?"

One reason I liked to run with Dave was that he never complained about my ten-minute-mile snail's pace. They say you should run slowly enough to be able to carry on a conversation. At that speed Dave and I could have read *War and Peace* to each other. We always topped off a morning jog with a fresh croissant at a little café famous for good strong coffee served with heavy cream.

But on this particular day Dave was picking me up, not for a run through Berkeley but for his sister's rehearsal dinner in Phoenix. He picked up my suitcase and threw it under the hood of his little yellow Volkswagen Bug. Dave had already been in Phoenix a week, helping his parents pick up out-of-town relatives, running errands, and generally smoothing out any wrinkles of panic that appeared. I plopped down on the front seat. He eyed my rumpled skirt and sweaty face.

"Kind of hot, isn't it? I'll take you to Gary and Joy's apartment so you can shower and rest. You and the other bridesmaids get to stay there. It's kind of small. They haven't moved in yet so there isn't very much furniture,

102

but—well, you know—it's kind of cute and it's home."

"Fine. I don't care if it's a grass shack as long as I can take a shower and relax. I've got a splitting headache."

Dave grinned. "Don't worry, you'll feel great after a shower."

He was right. I did feel great after a shower and even better after I had eaten a few dozen Swedish meatballs at the rehearsal dinner. Swedish meatballs along with Russian teacakes and shrimps hors d'oeuvres are the kind of food I love to "chain eat." They're just the perfect size to pop in your mouth one after another. That's fine if you stop at three or four but I seem to have the personality disorder known as "spareophobia": fear of leftovers. I can't stand to put anything away for another meal. I have to eat it all—now. Any dog at my place depending on table scraps for food would starve to death.

Finally, cursing the Swede who invented that dish, I proceeded with the others to rehearse the wedding. Everything went perfectly except for my continuous urge to belch as we walked down the aisle. I grabbed Dave's arm as we were walking out.

"I want to die. I'll never be able to look a Swedish meatball in the eye again."

"Do you want to run them off?"

"Now?"

"No, tomorrow morning. I'll pick you up around nine o'clock."

"Okay, but I'll have to run about forty-eight miles to burn them *all* off."

"No problem."

The next morning I was sitting out in front of the apartment when Dave pulled into the driveway. He hopped out of his car.

"How do you feel?" he asked.

"I have a meatball hangover. Don't talk so loud."

"Sorry. Let's get going. You'll love this run."

We ran slowly—a relaxed, easy pace—talking the whole way. We got to the foot of Camelback Mountain, a

Phoenix residential section. Quiet. It wasn't Berkeley. No pine or blossoming plum trees here. Giant saguaros stood in front yards: King Cactus. King over a whole variety of other cacti: prickly pears, innocent-looking woolly bears, beaver tails, and organ pipes. Bored Cadillacs sat in driveways. An LTD stared moodily past us. The air was warm and dry. No lawns either, just rocks and sand. I saw only one patch of green. Dave pointed out a swimming pool with the tile on the bottom set in the pattern of an American flag. We were rounding a corner when a man ran out to his driveway and called to the car pulling out, "And don't forget the vermouth and green olives!"

Wet martinis in the dessert. Extra dry wealth. A saguaro shrugged apathetically. We had been running uphill for the last twenty minutes and I didn't know if I could keep it up all the way to the top. I had visions of Dave and me breaking open a giant saguaro and drinking the juice, the way they do in the movies.

Everything was so *different* from Berkeley—like comparing chile con carne to pheasant under glass. *I* could just as well have been a Berkeley hippie asking for spare change! "Excuse me, sir, do you have any spare one-hundred dollar bills?"

We were heading for a castle made entirely of Camelback rock. Rumor had it that a crazy plastic surgeon or somebody had built it, getting so obsessed with it that his wife left him. I pictured their final scene:

"Harold darling, what do you say we picnic by the pool today—just you and I?"

"Not now, dear. I'm working on these plans for the south turret and then I have a three o'clock nose job."

"Then how about dessert tonight? We could have your favorite: root beer floats."

"Ah yes, Martha—the moat. Just how deep should I make the moat?"

"That does it, Harold! I'm leaving. You're obsessed with this castle."

"Yes, dear, I think you're right. The windows should be recessed."

It couldn't have been that easy. Real people are more interesting than that. By now I was getting tired.

"Let's walk for awhile," I gasped. I pointed to the castle. "What finally happened to him?"

"I think he still lives up there," Dave answered. We looked wonderingly up at the turrets and suddenly two little triangles appeared over the top. I couldn't figure it out until I saw paws appear. The two little triangles were German Shepherd ears.

I waved and called out, "Hi, pup."

Even from a hundred yards away I could see he had curled his lips the way dogs do when some bubble-head addresses them as "pup" or "boy." He watched us disapprovingly for a moment, then growled and disappeared.

I turned to Dave. "Remind me not to do that again."

The road wound around the hill and for awhile we lost sight of the castle. But there were other things to notice and I for one was still working on catching my breath. Every house had a car parked in the driveway: Jaguars, Porsches, many Cadillacs, a Mercedes or two. It looked like a posh desert car lot or an automobile breeding ground.

They say that at night, after children go to sleep, the toys wake up and play. I bet the same thing happens to cars. After they're parked for the night, they wake up and drive down the street or chat with the cars next door. Maybe they even gather at the corner and sit back on their hind wheels and trade stories about their owners.

"Oh, yeah, my present owner got divorced so she picked me up for a little comfort. She said she was going to drive me all over the desert or go to the club and just leave me parked out front. But I never get to go anywhere. She just sits in the house."

"I'd be remiss in my duties," says the Mercedes in a clipped accent, "if I neglected to point out that Americans simply have no understanding of how delicate we finer imports are . . ."

As usual, the Mercedes is interrupted by a Corvette: "Why, *delicate* is my middle name! I had such a pain in my upholstery—a sharp, stabbing pain. Didn't know what it could be until my owner realized that he left a screwdriver in his back pocket . . ."

I was jerked back into reality—or at least back to Phoenix—by a loud barking. I saw that we had come to the front of the castle. We crossed the street to get away from the dog and get a better view of the place. I was still puffing and wondering if our long uphill run had been worth it. I looked up, shading my eyes from the sun.

"It looks like something out of Disneyland," I said. "But I feel sort of let down—disappointed. I wonder if that's how that doctor felt after he built it. He put all that work into it and one good earthquake and he'd have just a rockpile on his hands."

"We don't have earthquakes in Phoenix."

"Well, you never know." I wiped the sweat off my face and turned to Dave. "Let's go back. I want to be sure I get in the shower and have plenty of time to get ready. We can't be late tonight."

The run home was easy, downhill all the way. We reached the apartment in less than twenty minutes, compared to the thirty-five it took us to get up there. We flung ourselves down on the front steps but Dave soon got up again.

"Hey, I'm hungry. Want a tangerine?" Without waiting for my answer he plucked some off the tree in the front yard. The entire area in front of the apartment building was dotted with citrus trees: lemon, orange, tangerine, and grapefruit. I was thirsty from the sun and the heat. The peels came off easily and the juicy segments burst inside my mouth. I found myself smiling involuntarily.

"These are great. Just what I needed."

Dave, his mouth full of fruit, nodded agreement. He knows me so well that most of the time I don't even have to say what I'm thinking or feeling. There was no need to speak then. There we sat, two friends, juice dripping out of our mouths, tired but grinning with almost unbearable contentment. For a moment I forgot that I was in Phoenix not to enjoy Dave but to celebrate Joy's wedding.

But Dave jumped up and said: "I'll pick you up at six o'clock tonight. In the meantime, just relax, will you? Everything is done. Joy is spending the day with Grandmother. You guys just take it easy."

"Okay, if you insist."

So the other bridesmaids and I spent the day relaxing and reading and swapping "Joy stories." Right on the dot at six o'clock I was arranging myself in Dave's Bug, trying not to wrinkle the voluminous folds of my burgundy dress, scuff my shoes, or sweat. I was nervous and excited and so was Dave.

"Can't you hurry up a little? You don't have to be that careful," he said.

"Shh. I don't want to create unsightly underarm stains!"

Dave sighed, waited till I gave him my Shirley Temple smile, then drove ninety miles an hour to the church. The other girls were behind us in a van driven by Dave's brother. He struggled to keep up with us and screeched to a stop behind the Bug in the church parking lot. He jumped out of the van and stalked over to us.

"Gee, Dave, couldn't you get it out of second gear?"

As it turned out, we were early, so there was plenty of time for me to sweat. Luckily the photographs were taken before the ceremony and none of them required us to raise our arms.

Joy looked beautiful. She was wearing the satin wedding gown her mother had made for her and she looked so tiny and petite—like one of those bride-and-groom cake ornaments. She could stand on her own cake, I thought to myself.

It was time. We were gathered at the back of the church in darkness, watching the candlelight flicker as the night breeze dressed in red roses and eucalyptus wafted down the aisle. We bridesmaids, who before two days ago had never met each other, were circled around Joy like sisters, united in our love for her.

Joy reached out and squeezed my hand. "Let's pray."

"Dear God, we ask that you would be glorified in this

ceremony, and we ask for a special blessing on Gary and Joy."

"We thank you, Lord, for your steadfast love and for the love that you have given them."

"Heavenly Father, I thank you that you have truly answered the desires of my heart and in your infinite wisdom have picked Gary to be my husband. I pray that you would help me meet his needs and that we would grow together toward you."

"God, thank you for choosing us to be your children. And I thank you for the way you've worked in Gary and Joy's lives. Bless this celebration as it points to you and your glory. And please make me stop sweating. Amen."

Before I knew it I was walking down the aisle, trying to remember to go slowly. I felt as if I were barely moving but later some joker asked if I thought I was in the Olympic heat for the 100-yard dash.

Then it was only Joy and her father walking slowly and calmly down the aisle. At times she smiled and nodded at people in the pews but for the most part her gaze was fixed on Gary as he stood at the altar waiting for her.

Suddenly my preoccupation with perspiration was gone and I was overwhelmed at the awesomeness of the occasion. Here were two people who were vowing not only to grow toward each other but to grow toward Christ together. I thought of the cars and swimming pools we had seen on Camelback Mountain and wondered what kind of promises those people had made. Joy's words broke in on my thoughts.

"All that I am is yours and all that I have is yours. I want to laugh, to cry, to grow with you. I love you with all the love that God has given me. Most of all, Gary, I want to reach toward Jesus with you more and more each day."

There it was. The greatest wedding gift of all: Jesus. When all the crystal is broken, the microwave blows up, and the car breaks down, they will still have the love of God. Someday, if one of them is standing alone without the other, Jesus Christ, who comes with an eternal guarantee, will still be with that one. The biggest house or the fastest car or the driest martini in the world will never give the "peace that passes all understanding."

I smiled. I had been smiling earlier that day but this time big tears were rolling down my cheeks. We laid our hands on Gary and Joy as the minister asked a special blessing on their life together.

I silently thanked God for all the Kleenex that I had thought to shove up the billowing sleeves of my dress. Joy looked up at me.

"My contact lenses are leaking," I whispered. She smiled and took a piece of tissue.

The minister pronounced them husband and wife. It was like uncorking a bottle of champagne. People were clapping and smiling and hugging each other. We at the altar all let out a sigh of relief, a joyous giggle or two, and joined in the smiling and hugging. The recessional was like a lilting dance; every step we took was a celebration of God's love.

In my excitement I dropped Kleenex all the way down the aisle. I still had a crumpled tissue in my hand. When I tried to blow my nose on it, it felt funny. It was a carnation.

Despite what magazine ads and
television commercials tell us,
nothing (no, not even a diamond)
lasts forever, except God. It's God's
love that is the most precious and
easiest to receive, yet often the least
recognized.

 **Checkout**

About God's love:

- It lasts forever (Romans chapter 8 says that **nothing** can separate us from the love of God, not even death.)
- It's unconditional (Not "I love you **if** you . . ." but "I love you.")
- It's returnable (We can love him back.)
- It comes in a lot of different packages: his creation, a phone call from a friend, a cup of tea, happy dreams

RUNNING A MARATHON!

If the body is a temple like the Bible says it is, mine:

- ☐ is slated for reconstruction
- ☐ needs a new paint job
- ☐ could withstand an earthquake of 6.0 on the Richter scale
- ☐ could blow away with the next breeze
- ☐ is up for a national architecture award

My mouth was full of chocolate birthday cake and my dad was proposing a toast to me with a cup of French roast when the call came.

"Debbie, quick! It's Lyn calling long distance from Hawaii to wish you happy birthday." Mom, being closest to the phone, had answered and as usual was reminding me that it was long distance—as though I thought Honolulu was a San Francisco suburb. I climbed over my grandmother and assorted neighbors who were crammed around the table in my parents' kitchen. I managed of course to knock over the cream and step on the dog, which isn't all that surprising since she's a small, brown chihuahua who blends into the pattern on the linoleum.

The first thing Lynie said when I picked up the phone was: "Why is Suki yelping?"

"Oh, I managed to step on her," I answered, wiping chocolate from my mouth.

"Well, happy birthday, you turkey! Are you having a good one? What's going on?"

"Oh, you know, the usual small, intimate birthday dinner—half the neighborhood is here. Mom made chicken cacciatore, pasta with pesto sauce, garlic bread, marinated artichokes, steamed broccoli, and three-bean salad. And oh yes, frittata as an appetizer and," I said, licking my fingers, "chocolate cake with chocolate mint icing."

"Ugh, gross." Lynie hates any form of mint, chocolate or otherwise. I think her hatred began when, at the age of three, she ate two packs of peppermint gum and threw up. She shuns all forms of mint, from juleps to antacids. It amazes me that she manages to use toothpaste.

"Well," I said defensively, "*I* think it's delicious. And so does everybody else. So what's new with you?"

"Dan thinks you should come out here in December and that all three of us should run the Honolulu marathon."

"What? That sounds fantastic! But a little expensive." My parents of course were listening intently.

"Sydney," my mother said, "I don't like the sound of this."

"But imagine the thrill of it," I said. "Of course I've heard of people dropping dead afterward."

My mother was drumming her fingers on the table. She leaned over to my father. "I don't like this one bit—it's expensive and it's dangerous."

"I think we can do it," Lyn said. "You've been running regularly and we have nine months to train."

I laughed into the phone. "Nine months? Might as well just get pregnant."

"Debra!" My mother jumped up but my father pulled her back into her chair.

"Nah, this is better," Lyn assured me, "you're not fat after running it, and there's no diapers to change."

"Good point," I answered. "Let's do it."

By this time my mom had her head down on the table and was clutching her empty wine glass. "The last time she said 'Let's do it!' they jumped off the roof."

My dad was patting her on the back. "Don't worry, honey. They're adults now—I think."

We hung up, after promising to send postcards to each other with our weekly mileage, and vowing to run the whole race together. I turned to my family.

"I'm so excited. I can't wait."

"Break it to us gently," my father warned.

"Lynie and I are going to run the Honolulu marathon. Wow, twenty-six big ones!"

"Oh," my mother moaned, "today you're twenty-five. You'll never make twenty-six. Will I never have grandchildren? Why do you want to do this?"

"Just to say I've done it. It'll be such a thrill."

"You had your tonsils out—wasn't that thrilling enough?"

"C'mon, Mom. Lyn and I are going to do this together. The last time we did anything together was when I was eleven. We suffered through two months of practicing and memorizing 'Peter and the Wolf' and 'Flight of the Bumble Bee.' Then, right after our recital, we tore up the sheet music and never played either one again."

Mother stared vacantly off into space. "I always did like those pieces. Why don't you take up piano again instead?"

Dad broke in. "I think the marathon's a great idea. Let's drink a toast to the girls. All the way. Twenty-six miles!" He stood and lifted his coffee mug. He's fond of making toasts and had made five or six already, so it was a good thing that everybody had switched to coffee.

"Thanks, Dad." I hugged him and turned to Mom.

"I guess I'm outnumbered," she sighed. "I just hope you don't get big calf muscles like your cousin Sheila did when she ran track in high school."

"Mom, Sheila was *born* with big calf muscles."

"Maybe so. Now, how about some more cake?"

"Great." I was about to hand her my plate when I stopped abruptly. "No, Mom. Sorry. I'm in training now." Mom sighed again and put the cake away. At that moment I became a marathon runner.

Never having run more than seven or eight miles before, I consulted a friend of mine about how to train. She was an exercise physiologist and a seasoned marathon runner herself.

"You don't need to kill yourself," Ellen advised. "There's no need to increase your mileage more than ten percent a week. And you don't have to run every single day. Your body needs time to recover."

"What's the longest I should run before the race?"

"You don't have to run more than eighteen or twenty miles at the maximum. In a race you can theoretically run three times your training distance. So if you knew you could do fifteen miles, you could do a marathon."

"You mean you do the last eleven miles on sheer guts?"

"You could say that," she said hesitantly. "I try to avoid that attitude, though, because then people start thinking they can get by with minimum training, say ten miles. But running sixteen more miles on sheer guts is asking too much of your guts."

So we sat down with my Sierra Club calendar and mapped out my schedule. It was pretty basic. A hard day followed by an easy day with a long, slow run on the weekends, and Sunday off. It wasn't bad at all until summer came. By then my morning runs were up to about nine miles. If I got up at exactly 5:30 a.m., threw in my contact lenses and dressed in six minutes, I could run and make it to work by eight o'clock. Since I was determined to be a marathon runner I could live with that. What I couldn't live with was only five or six hours of sleep. I would find

---

Getting started

If you've never exercised before and want to get started, here are a few tips:

- Choose an activity that you **enjoy**, no use forcing yourself to do something you positively **hate**

- Warm up with a few simple stretches: leg stretches, side-bends, arm circles

- Do at least 20 minutes of aerobic exercise (where you're sweating and breathing hard) at least 3 times per week

- Cool down with stretching for at least 10 minutes after an aerobic work-out

myself yawning and staring at my watch at 8:30 p.m., preparing to leave wherever I was by nine o'clock. My friends would nod knowingly and say, "Oh, are you expecting an important phone call?"

"Well . . . no," I would say ruefully.

"Then you're going home to watch that TV Movie of the Week?"

"Uh, no."

Then they would grab my arm and look intently in my eyes. "Aren't you feeling well?"

"I feel great. I'm going home to go to bed."

"At nine o'clock! Sorry we're so boring."

"No, it's not that. I have to get up at 5:30 to run, so I need my sleep." I lost most people after "get up at 5:30."

My social life suffered from all that training, but my spiritual life was blossoming. I was now spending anywhere from one to two hours running with God. I felt his presence more keenly than ever before. After about an hour of running, colors seemed brighter and more vivid. Trees and birds looked sharper and sounds were more intense. It was as if my fine tuning was being adjusted to bring God in loud and clear. Long runs gave me more time to listen to God and not just talk. Some people might

---

Getting started

If you've never been spiritually fit before and want to get started, here are a few tips:

- Find a church that you **enjoy** attending, no use forcing yourself to go somewhere you positively **hate**
- Warm up with a few simple exercises: start reading scripture (one of the New Testament Gospels is a good place to begin), think about what you've read, tell God what's on your heart and mind, and listen to him
- Have a two-way conversation with God every day and get together with other Christians to share and encourage each other, not just Sundays but in the week too
- When making choices throughout the day, cultivate your God-consciousness by asking yourself, "What would Jesus want me to do?" Unwind at the end of the day by going over the choices you made and lifting them up to God

explain it away physiologically as a "surge of beta-endorphins" but I knew better.

Lynie and I continued to send postcards back and forth across the Pacific. Some were wordy: Lyn: I had the best eight-mile run today (Sat). Ran up in Tilden Park around ten o'clock this morning. I could smell the sun on the grass. Reminded me of riding our bikes early on a summer morning in our shorts and tennis shoes.

Others were short: Deb: Humidity unbearable. Ran ten miles around Canal and Diamond Head. I wanted to die. Lynie.

Fall brought colder, darker morning runs. I still ran in shorts but with a jacket and gloves and the realization that the race was now only three months away. It was hard getting up on those foggy mornings with just my radio to bid me goodbye.

I still preferred running alone, with only God for company, waving at a few cruising police cars or white-shirted milkmen. On those cool, misty mornings I learned who wore suit and tie to work, who wore steel-toed boots, who carried a briefcase, who carried a black lunch box. I learned who were working women (I could see them, fully dressed, drinking coffee in their kitchens) and who were housewives (they came out in their bathrobes to pick up the morning paper), but in the dawn's stillness they seemed the same. Maybe that was because of all those neatly trimmed squares of lawn that they had in common. Some people waved and some didn't. Some even said "good morning." I wondered which of them knew Jesus, who didn't, and who was looking for him.

On Thanksgiving Day I was late for turkey dinner. I was out on a twelve-mile run, giving thanks the whole way. I can't honestly say I spent the entire two hours in direct conversation with God, but I was constantly aware of his presence.

I slid into my place at the table, hair still wet from my shower and my cheeks probably still flushed from running. It was pointed out to me that the mashed potatoes had gotten hard and cold. I mumbled an apology.

Dad said grace. Then I enjoyed the best Thanksgiving dinner I ever had. Guiltlessly I reveled in the glory of turkey, stuffing, cranberry sauce, biscuits, yams, and salad. I skipped the cold mashed potatoes. Mom brought out dessert: fresh pumpkin pie smothered with whipped cream. I cut myself a piece.

"I already gave your father a piece," my mom said.

"I know. This is for me." My mother stared as I wolfed down the pie. "Mom," I said, my mouth crammed full, "I just burned off 1,200 calories."

"I don't care if you just burned the house down. You're going to look like a pig if you keep eating like that."

I shook my head and finished my pie. Well, one benefit of running long distance was dropping twenty pounds.

It wasn't just the exercise, though. Every time I ran I sensed the power of Jesus Christ. And Jesus' power and involvement in my life was becoming more obvious to me these days, in lots of practical ways. If he could give me strength to go up a hill he could give me strength to resist dessert. But it was more than that. Realizing that God actually loves me was the key to my weight problem. My secret fear was of not being loved. I starved myself for days out of panic that I wouldn't be loved unless I was thin, and then binged for weeks.

But Jesus loves me whatever my size or shape. When I finally understood that, not just in my head but in my heart, the problem faded away. The fat didn't, right away —but I had been carrying that fear, and that fat, for twenty-five years. Only gradually did I see that Jesus died for me without making any demands. He isn't standing at the gates of heaven holding out a pair of jeans and saying: "No one comes to the Father but by Calvin Kleins, size nine."

He doesn't require thinness or good grades or perfect skin before he'll love me. He simply loves me. That's what destroyed my fear and the obsessive eating that had consoled me. It was that knowledge that made me smile to myself every morning as I ran.

I'm still known for my occasional overdoses on

chocolate or Thanksgiving dinners, but now it's the exception instead of the rule.

At one point that winter I told my pastor that I wanted to make sure I was going to make it the whole twenty-six miles so I had written on my entry form that I was running for my church. He laughed. But the Sunday before I left, somewhere between singing "Great God, We Sing Your Mighty Hand" and "Alas! And Did My Savior Bleed?" he called me forward to accept a T-shirt from the congregation with the words "Berkeley Covenant Church" emblazoned on the back. I was slightly embarrassed but greatly pleased and completely humbled by the faith my "family" had in me.

A few days later my friend Dave drove me to the airport. Packed in my suitcase was my marathon shirt, a pile of cards wishing me good luck and Merry Christmas, and my marathon number, 203. The last thing Dave said before I got on the plane was: "Remember, we'll still love you even if you don't finish."

When the plane touched down in Honolulu, instead of leaping up from my seat I found myself paralyzed with the realization that two years ago I was doing exactly the same thing: arriving in Hawaii to stay with Lyn and Dan. But this time I was strong and smiling and filled with a new zest for life that knowing God had given me. During the two years that had passed I had grown stronger in more ways than one. This race was more than just a physical performance for me. It was also a symbol of steady and sometimes painful spiritual growth and knowledge of God.

I looked down the aisle. I wasn't the only runner on board. Scores of waffle and ripple-soled running shoes were heading for the exit. I got up and took a deep breath. It was four days before the race, too late to train now.

"The hay is in the barn," Ellen had said to me the day before. This was it. Lynie was waiting for me and we hugged silently.

"Are you ready?" I whispered.

"I don't know. I guess so. Are you?"

"Yes. No—I don't know. I'm scared."

"So am I."

We pulled away from each other and I stared at her face.

"Good grief," I finally said, "you'd think we were going to war." It had been so long since we'd seen each other but here we were, worried about a silly race.

"Lynie! I'm so glad to see you."

"Me too." We hugged again but this time noisily—talking at the same time, giggly and teary-eyed. We laughed all the way home, partly from happiness, partly from nervousness, but mostly because Lynie was just learning to drive a non-automatic and the car would buck across each intersection when she let out the clutch.

The night before the race we loaded up on carbohydrates: spaghetti, garlic bread, salad, peach pie, and of course some chocolate bars I insisted on eating, for good luck if for nothing else.

The race started at 6 a.m. so we turned in at ten o'clock that night. We realized our mistake at going to bed so early after five trips to the bathroom, two glasses of iced tea and a glass of milk between the three of us. It was one o'clock before I recognized the even, steady breathing of sleep coming from their room.

I wandered out onto that balcony I had stood on two years before. The air was warm and moist. Saturday sounds of late night parties drifted up past my seventh floor perch and were swallowed up by the night sky.

"God," I prayed, "just help us to finish this race and somehow glorify you."

Inside again, I picked up my race number and examined it carefully. Number 203, Honolulu Marathon. "In the Footsteps of the King's Runners." Which king? I knew who my King was.

We left at 5 a.m. Eight of us crowded into a little blue Monza. It was already 72 degrees and humid and we stuck to each other like slices of cheese. We peeled ourselves apart as we got out of the car, somewhere near the start. Dan and his friends, much faster runners than Lyn and I were, lined up toward the front of the crowd. She and I went to find our places in the back.

Then, as any eight-year-old on the first day of school will tell you, just before you're about to do something monumental you have to get to a toilet. It is much simpler if you are an eight-year-old at school than it is when you are surrounded by seven thousand other runners all with the same idea.

The lines at the portable toilets were miles long so Lynie and I searched for another suitable spot. We weren't the only ones. People were wandering around, ducking into doorways, sliding into sideyards, and crawling around cars. We found a very tiny space between a brick wall and a Volkswagen. I'm sure nobody saw us, but I am quite sure they heard us wheezing with laughter. Had I trained for nine months and flown 5,000 miles to relieve myself between a brick wall and a foreign car?

We sobered up as soon as we took our places in the pack, checked our hair clips, and straightened our shorts. Lynie's church had given her a T-shirt, too. It read "Kalihi Union Church" on the front. On the back were the words *Everybody Needs Love* with a picture of a milk carton that read: *GOD: Everlasting Drink, fortified with Jesus. Unlimited fl. oz.*

It was a pitch black morning but precisely at 6 a.m. came a roar from the cannon and the sky was lit up with fireworks bursting overhead. Shades of the "Star Spangled Banner"! Lyn and I were screaming with excitement. In fact everyone seemed to be screaming, shouting something, or laughing. We didn't actually start running for about ten minutes. Then we were doing it. We were running a marathon.

The first aid station was near the zoo. It smelled of zoo. I was not excited at that point to drink water or defizzed Coke. But I remembered the warning Ellen had given me: "Drink at every station," so I reluctantly accepted a paper cup of cold water and an icy sponge.

We had gone only about three miles and already my shirt was soaked with perspiration. The next twelve miles breezed by. Lynie and I talked about the weird sensation of drinking flat Coke while trying to run, and about a lot of more important things. We chatted about Christmas and what did you get for Mom and Dad?

"By the way," Lyn said, "Dan's grandfather lives right on the course. He said he'd be watching for us."

I nodded. I had met the old gentleman once.

We ran past giant speakers blaring out the theme from "Rocky," little old ladies playing ukeleles, and small children all lined up clapping and cheering. Each cheer and each smile was like a shot of energy—instant adrenalin. My feet felt lighter and breathing came easier for at least a quarter mile past that crowd.

After mile nineteen I could feel the fatigue set in. I wouldn't say that I "hit the wall" but my feet started to ache and I couldn't cool off. That's when Lynie stopped talking. All she would say was: "Yup." Our conversation was reduced to reminders.

"Keep your arms down."

"Yup."

"Keep drinking."

"Yup."

"Keep breathing."

The five miles down Kalanianiole Highway seemed endless. We had already run that stretch on the way out and now we were running the same road back again. I felt as if I was having a bad dream. In the same way that promises are made in the heat of battle, promises are made while running a marathon. Suddenly "Peter and the Wolf" and the "Flight of the Bumble Bee" seemed very attractive to me. I vowed to take up piano again.

I looked down at my legs. Funny, they looked like legs, but they didn't feel like legs. They felt like wet sacks of flour, chugging up and down. My mind was unable to think in linear sentences. Bits and pieces of past conversations floated in and out of my brain. Sheer guts. Neither of us had run more than fifteen miles before and now we were past that. I looked at Lyn, her face down, concentrating on every step.

121

"We're running on sheer guts."

She looked up at me sober and serious. "No," she said, "somebody just spilled some Coke."

I sighed. I was having fantasies of a cool Berkeley breeze coming through the palm trees, wafting past the plumeria and colored crotons and over my steaming body. I also vowed never to complain about San Francisco fog again.

My feet were making their own vows. They were doing an impersonation of raw hamburger meat. Somebody had put ground beef in my running shoes.

"Alas! And Did My Savior Bleed?" Nailed to a cross. We'll still love you even if you don't finish. Please, God, help us to finish.

Then, coming down Kahala Avenue, mile twenty-three, there was Dan's Grandpa, hearing aids in both ears, perched on top of a six-foot ladder in his front yard. I was never so happy to see anyone in all my life.

"Go, girls!" he shouted. "That's my daughters out there running! Number 203 and 646!" He was yelling and pointing at us. I was afraid he would fall off the ladder.

"Hi, Grandpa!" We waved and smiled. All smiles—had we made a mistake? Was this the beginning of the race instead of the end? I felt great. We went striding past Grandpa and his neighborhood cheering section that held a sign that read: "Go Danny, Lyn, and Debbie." That touched me. I was not even a part of their family and they were rooting for me, too. We were laughing now, our heads held high. As we put that group behind us, though, our laughter turned into that sound that was something between a sob and a choke.

"Did you see Grandpa?" Lynie asked. "That was Grandpa."

Since he claimed me as a daughter I was not above claiming him as my grandfather. "Yes, I saw him. I saw Grandpa. He's great." We said a few more incoherent things about Grandpa.

Just then we passed two men, maybe twenty-two years old, walking and glistening with sweat.

"Look at them," I heard one of them say. "How can they keep going?"

The other one pointed to our shirts. "I guess they have God on their side." Lynie and I looked at each other and smiled.

Our energy spurt was brief. Up until that point the sky had been cloudy, the sun kept back from doing any real harm. Just as we started up Diamond Head Road, two miles to the finish line, the sun came out, blazing down on us without mercy. Lyn, being acclimated, could do a little better in the heat than I could. I thought I was dying.

"Oh," I moaned, "I feel like a turkey on a spit. A big, fat, roasted turkey going round and round past the coals. A turkey with lead drumsticks and hot rubber wings. A turkey with . . ."

"Would you shut up and quit talking about food?" She was right. We were runners. Runners in the footsteps of the King.

I accepted another cold sponge from the last aid station. It was full of cool water.

And then we were over the top of Diamond Head Road and ahead of us was Kapiolani Park and the finish line and water and stopping and cheering and cheering and cheering.

You would have thought we were winning the Olympics. As we neared the chutes I grabbed Lynie's hand. Our time: 5:48—five hours and forty-eight minutes, three and a half hours after the first place runner. We went through the chutes together, laughing, crying, and holding hands.

Every finisher is a winner they say, so we were winners. Officials placed shell leis around our necks and then the rain poured down—furiously and suddenly, without warning.

Who cared? We were winners.

That race was over, but not our training with God. We're still runners in the marathon—runners for God's King.

 **Checkout**

Physical fitness

How do I think about my body? In terms of fitness, or whether my clothes fit "nice"?

Being "fit" is being "healthy" and that doesn't necessarily mean having a body like a fashion model. What does being physically "fit" mean? It means being ready to go. And that means endurance, strength, and flexibility. How do you rate?

Yes   No

☐ Can you run a couple of miles without having to have an ☐ ambulance ready and waiting?

☐ Are you strong enough to carry 23 record albums up two ☐ flights of stairs?

☐ Can you touch your toes without bending your knees? ☐

Spiritual fitness

Being spiritually "fit" is similar to being physically fit—same principles: endurance, strength, and flexibility. How do you rate?

Yes   No

☐ Can you hang in there and trust God when there seems ☐ to be no end in sight?

☐ Are you strong enough to stand up for what you believe, ☐ to help people out in a crisis, and have faith in the face of tragedy?

☐ Can you adjust and adapt to the unexpected, even if ☐ it's not the way you wanted things to turn out?